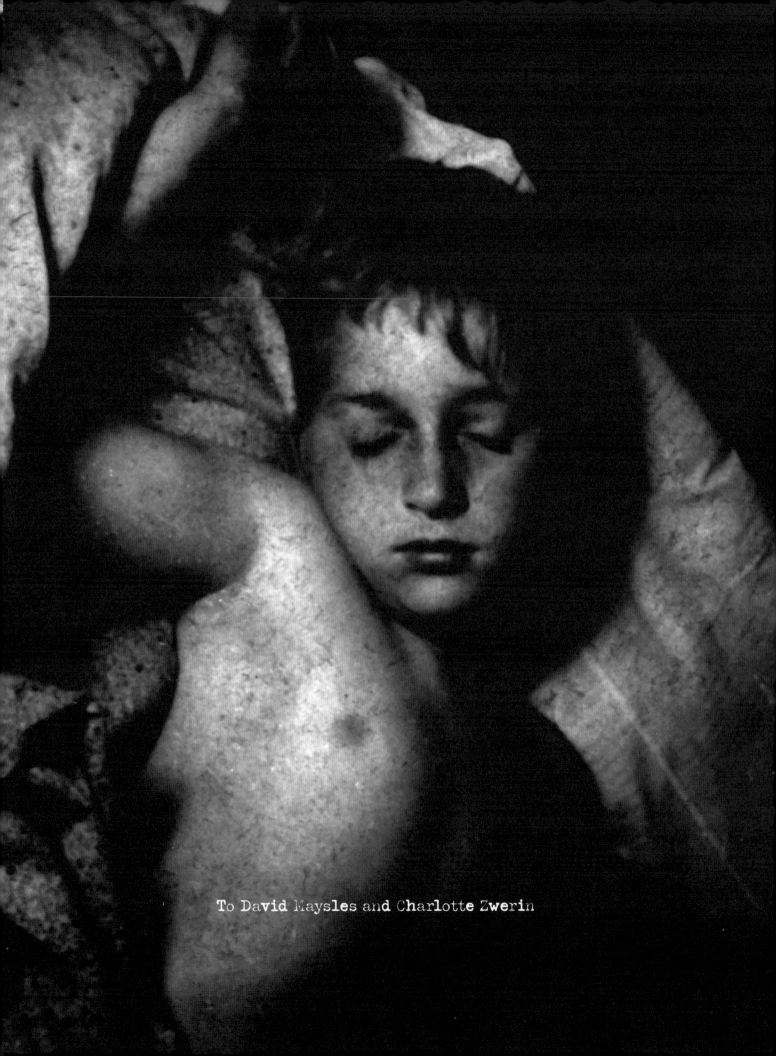

To David Maysles and Charlotte Zwerin

edited by michael chaiken

steven kasher and sara maysles

albert maysles

A MAYSLES
SCRAPBOOK

photographs/cinemagraphs/
documents

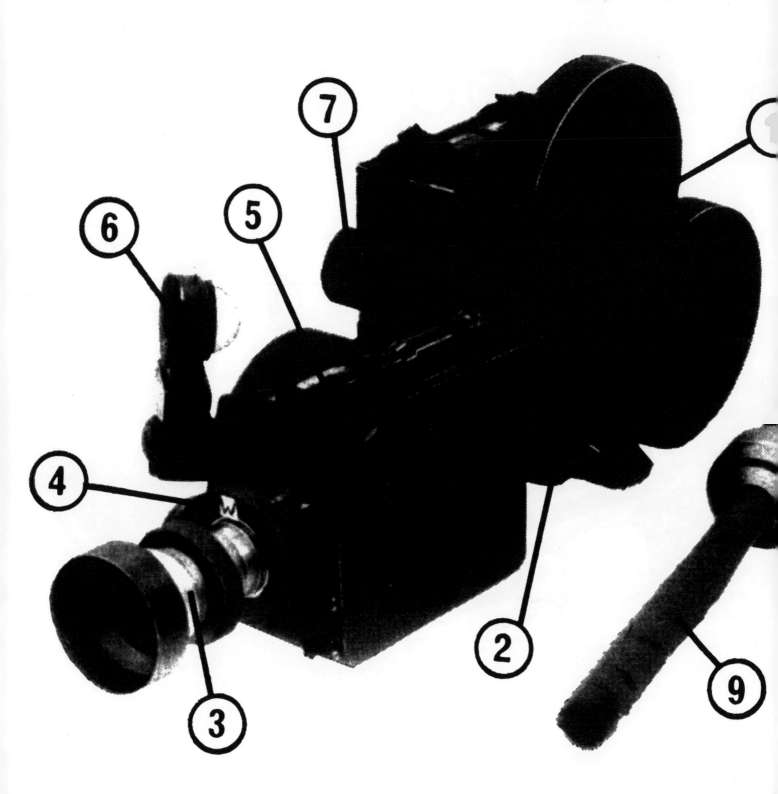

Custom-built camera (left) is basically a 16-mm Auricon with its interchangeable film magazine **1** shifted from top to back for better balance. Shoulder-rest **2** is rubber-padded. Zoom lens **3** is an interchangeable 17→68-mm Angenieux; letter **4** indicates zoom position so that tape recordist can tell what area is being covered. Reflex finder **5** is angled so that its cup fits naturally over eye. Incident-light meter **6** is fastened on camera. Film

HIS EQUIPMENT

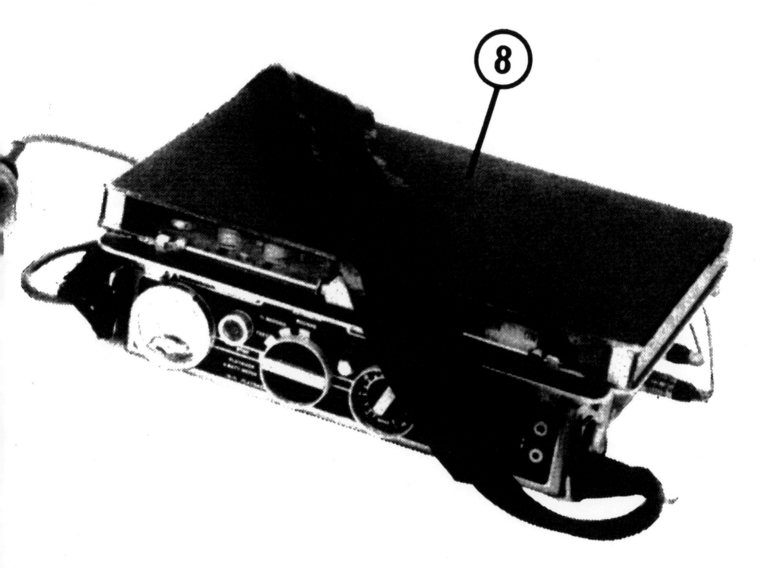

take-up torque is adjustable **7,** to compensate for variables, such as temperature. Tape recorder is a Nagra, with its deck **8** extended to accommodate 7- instead of 5-in. reels. It has a 60-cycle tuning fork, registering a pulse signal on the tape for sound synchronization. The ElectroVoice 642 microphone is shielded with Acoustofoam **9** to tone down its appearance, so that it won't be too conspicuous; this material also adds some wind protection.

Foreword
by Martin Scorsese

AL MAYSLES ONCE QUOTED ORSON WELLES as a way of describing his own aspirations as a filmmaker: "The camera person should have an eye behind the camera that is the eye of a poet."

So let *me* quote Welles, on De Sica's *Shoeshine*, as a way of describing Al's *achievements* as a filmmaker: "What De Sica can do, I can't do . . . The camera disappeared, the screen disappeared, it was just life."

"It was just life." That's how I felt when I saw Robert Drew's *Primary*, shot by Al and Ricky Leacock, for the first time. Like the extraordinary films Al later made with his brother David—*Salesman, Gimme Shelter, Grey Gardens*—this was a truly eye-opening experience, a real drama unfolding in real time. I was gripped by these pictures, by the force of their apparently simple images. And I realized right away that there was an extraordinary keenness of perception at work behind the camera, a sense of discretion but also a burning desire to grasp life in all its complexity—its beauty and its ugliness, its joy and its sorrow, all at once. In fact, I can attest to this based on personal experience.

I once had a job as Al's assistant, and I had to "aim" or "focus" lights as needed. It was a tough job—I had to follow, even anticipate, his every move, and I could see how attuned he was to the world before his camera. It was like watching a master paint.

Al truly does have the eye of a poet. Which is ultimately what makes the camera disappear, and give way to life.

There are many films these days—documentary and fiction—in which the director and the cameraman *imagine* that they're merging with their subjects, letting the camera disappear. But that's not the case. Since the advent of lightweight DV cameras, there's a lot of what is now called "run and gun" filmmaking. The camerawork is certainly "dynamic," but there's little sense of a relationship between the cameraman and the people.

WHEN AL IS BEHIND THE CAMERA, there's a sensitivity to mood, to space and light, to the energy between the people in the room. The camera is an inquisitive presence, but also a *loving* presence, an *empathic* presence, tuned to the most sensitive emotional vibrations. This is partly a reflection of Al's own temperament as a person, because there are few people in the business of filmmaking as thoughtful and as sensitive—rare qualities in any field, but especially rare in this one. But beyond that, it's a reflection of his temperament as an artist. And his greatness.

This wonderful book offers a record in images of Al's life as a human being and as an artist—the same thing, really. A beautifully assembled scrapbook, but also a living record. Because Al Maysles' images are alive in a way that few ever even hope to be.

Introduction
by Albert Maysles

AS A PHOTOGRAPHER AND DOCUMENTARIAN
I happily place my fate and faith in reality. Reality is my caretaker, the provider of subjects, themes, experiences—all endowed with the power of truth and the romance of discovery. The closer I adhere to reality the more honest and authentic my tales. After all, knowledge of the real world is exactly what we need to better understand and, possibly, to love one another. It's my way of making the world a better place.

There is a moment in *Salesman* when the main character, Paul Brennan, has been having a rough day. He takes a break, retiring to a cafeteria where he sits just staring off into the blue. There is nothing to interrupt his thinking—as we meditate on his suffering. So, while the motion picture thrives on motion and sound, at times the pause of stillness and silence elicits the most powerful reflection.

The photograph is a moment all the more engaging for lack of motion and sound. Both photography and cinema can bring the viewer so close to what is happening that the experience of the subject can become that of the viewer. Photography came first for me, at age ten or eleven when I bought my first camera—ever so tiny and for just 35 cents. At age 27 I traveled around Europe with a borrowed Leica and at age 28 traveled to Russia with Leica and a 16 mm Keystone wind-up movie camera. Six years later I built my own 16 mm camera.

From the start my greatest asset has been my love for people, which has helped me get access to them and render a true picture, unprejudiced by a point of view. As my mother used to put it, "there's good in everybody." I'm determined to film the good, as well as—with discretion—moments of vulnerability.

In conversation with me, a distinguished *New York Times* correspondent mentioned that his favorite word was "random". Also mine, I thought, but with some variation: instead of "random" I would use the expression "by chance" but it is not by chance alone. When I am filming it is the real thing as long as I don't exercise control over what is happening. But the camera needs something else: what Orson Welles has described as "the eye of the poet behind the lens." I am reminded of a walk I took years ago with the renowned photographer Bruce Davidson. Each time he took a shot the picture was what I could have taken if only I had noticed it.

In a later visit with Bruce I met up with Henri Cartier-Bresson and showed him film footage I had shot in a railroad station in Moscow. As the train came to a stop at an empty platform suddenly all doors flung open and a great flood of people covered the platform as they approached the camera. Henri leapt into the air applauding and cheering.

Over the years I've found elements of my own experience—especially from childhood—cropping up in one form or another in the films I've made. In grammar school hardly a day would go by without an Irish kid picking a fight with me because I was Jewish. Filming the four Irish Bible salesmen gave me the opportunity to put down my fists and come to true and lasting friendships.

As a child I was so taken by watching my father's facial expressions as we listened to good music. That was a most beautiful course in music appreciation. Years later I filmed the Rolling Stones and then Vladimir Horowitz listening to the playback of their own music. I fastened my focus on their hands and faces, bringing the viewer so much closer to the music.

The films themselves have become tools for teaching how to make documentaries and understand the world around us. Each film is an entertainment. Each is an examination of matters such as everyday life (*Salesman*), the mother-daughter relationship (*Grey Gardens*), poverty (*Lalee's Kin*). And there's plenty more to come.

I'm pleased to put forth these photographs and cinemagraphs, prints made from the original film footage. Many of these have been, until now, dear to me alone. Now I hope these images will also find a welcome place in the eyes and hearts of my readers.

16

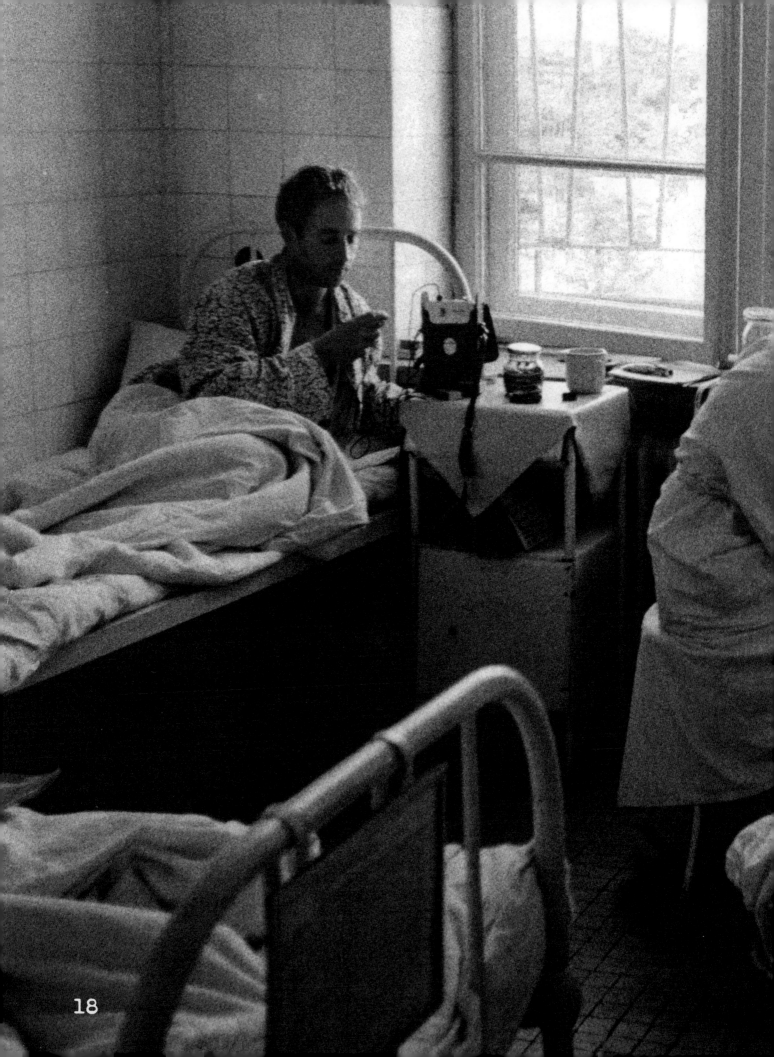

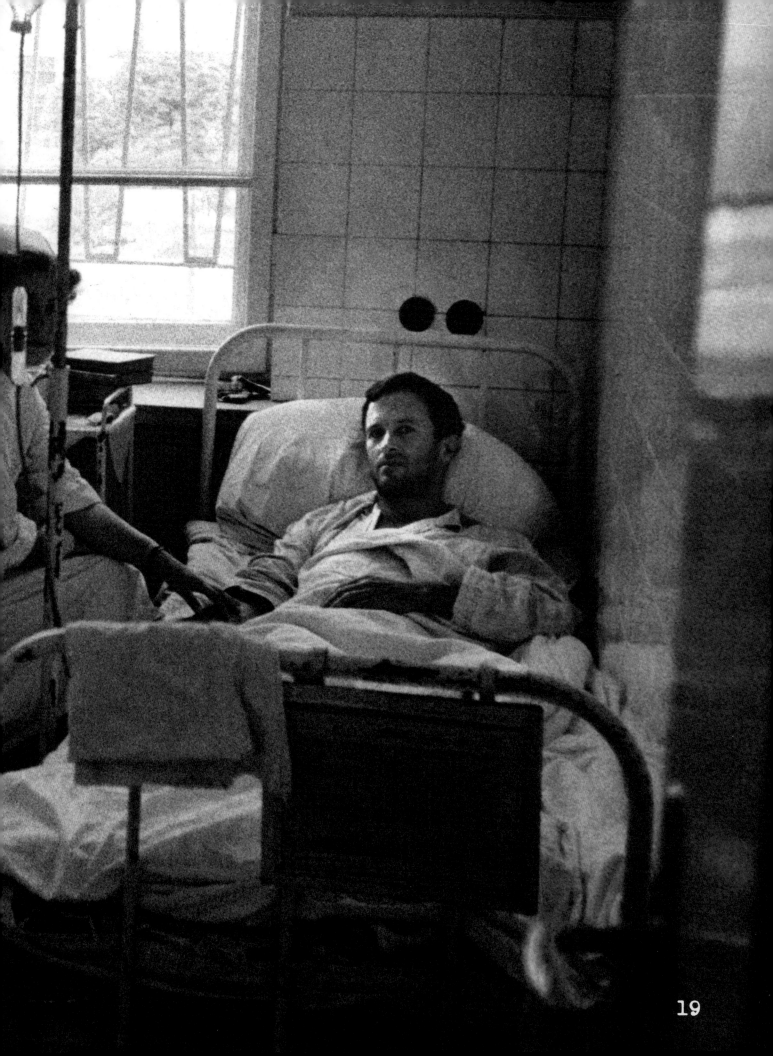

19

SIMMONS COLLEGE

BOSTON 15, MASSACHUSETTS

———

DIVISION OF
PHILOSOPHY, PSYCHOLOGY, AND EDUCATION

STEPHEN R. DEANE, Chairman

Autobiography of Albert Maysles

My father was a government postal clerk and my mother is a school teacher. I also have a brother and sister.

I myself am an Instructor in Psychology at Simmons College, Boston. From 1952 to 1955 I was a full time Instructor in Social Relations at Boston University where I now am a candidate for PhD in Psychology. I hold two degrees in Psychology--a B.A. from Syracuse University in 1949 and an M.A. from Boston University in 1952. I have also done research work on the psychophysiology of emotions in 1949-1950 at the Boston Psychopathic Hospital. I also served a two year appointment at the Masschusetts General Hospital as Research Fellow and at the same hospital headed a research project investigating sleep, drugs, and hypnosis in their interrelations.

The summer of 1955 I spent a month in the Soviet Union. About a week of that time was spent inspecting 3 mental hospitals in the Moscow Area. I have written of these experiences, one article, "Russian Mental Hospitals" appearing in the January edition of the Boston University Graduate Journal; another article, "Russian close-up" appearing in the April edition of the same journal. This fall a paper that I read to an international conference on mental hospital care will appear in the publication of the conference proceedings. The paper concerned my visits to the mental hospitals. My lectures on the Soviet Union have included Harvard University, Boston University, the Library for Intercultural Studies, and many lay groups.

I feel that these illustrated lectures and publications have made some contributions to strengthening the ties of mutual friendship between the peoples of both countries.

I am also an experienced photographer and am preparing a picture-book to be published this fall on the Soviet Union

✳✳✳✳✳✳✳✳✳✳✳✳✳✳✳✳✳✳✳✳✳✳✳✳✳

Preferred date of arrival: June 15, 1965

Place of Entry: Czechoslovakia

Subway Thinking

Wedding Ring

Architect
& Draftsman

Constructi
Worke

Moscow Hellion

Somewhat
Suspicious

Moscow City
Court

Sunday at t
Park

Self- Entertainment

Medical student

Subway Worker & Student

24

26

31

RUSSIAN CLOSE-UP

ALBERT MAYSLES

Psychologist at Simmons College. He recently spent 30 days in Russia. Met top leaders, hundreds of average Russians. First American to see and photograph the 3 mental hospitals he inspected.

Lecturer, author, photographer.

Completely Uncensored Movie Film
and Lecture by

ALBERT MAYSLES

First Intimate and Panoramic View
of Everyday Life in Russia

A Social Psychologist Shows You
the Human Side
We Have Not Seen

Russians

Walking . . .

on the street . . . in the subways . . . in the Kremlin

Working . .

at building construction . . . at the Moscow Auto Works . . . on a collective farm . . .

32

Buying and Selling . . .

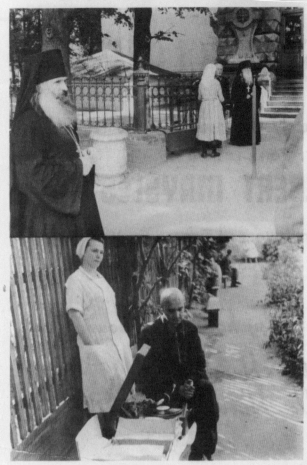

Playing . .

jump-rope in a backyard . . .

soccer at Dynamo Stadium . . .

Ballet at the Bolshoi Theatre

Praying . .

In churches . . .

in synagogues

In Trouble

Inside mental hospitals . . .

at court trials

Photographs by Albert Maysles

ALL KINDS OF PEOPLE: Muscovites, Uzbeki, Turkestani, Mongolians

OF ALL AGES AND OCCUPATIONS:

Swaddled infants, children with sand pails, school children in uniform, athletes, teachers, workers, housewives, psychiatrists, lawyers, ice cream vendors . . .

Lectured at . . .

Radcliffe College, Boston University, Intercultural Library, New York. Women's Clubs, Church groups, etc.

What People have said . . .

LAUREN BROWN, President United Nations Council, Radcliffe College.

"'Pictures were excellent . . . an enjoyable and informative presentation of some of the little publicized conditions of how the people really live and feel."

WILLIAM J. PINARD, Professor Boston University.

"In my opinion Mr. Maysles excels in the qualities necessary to instruct and entertain an audience. He has a pleasing personality and his poise, springing from knowledge and intellectual integrity, is excellent. His portrayal of conditions in Russia made a profound impression on me not only because of the intimate details revealed but also, and more especially, because of the objectivity and reliability of the material presented."

CLIFTON DANIELS — in The New York Times — August 24, 1955.

". . . Soviet party chiefs . . . met Albert Maysles, Instructor in Psychology . . . During the reception, (he) chatted across the table with the Presidium members . . . Mr. Pervukhin (First Deputy Prime Minister) told Mr. Maysles his wish to see Soviet mental hospitals would be granted. . ."

MARGUERITE HIGGINS in the New York Herald Tribune, October 3, 1955.

"As good an example as any of how individual American enterprise can pay off even in proletarian Russia is the case of Albert Maysles, psychology teacher at Boston University . . . (who) recently found himself touring Soviet hospitals for the mentally ill that had never before been visited by Westerners; addressing large audiences over the Moscow radio, and interviewing leading Soviet psychiatrists . . . the Russians could scarcely have treated Mr. Maysles better had he been officially designated as a member of a governmental delegation."

33

Photographs currently appearing in the Christian Science Monitor and Boston Globe

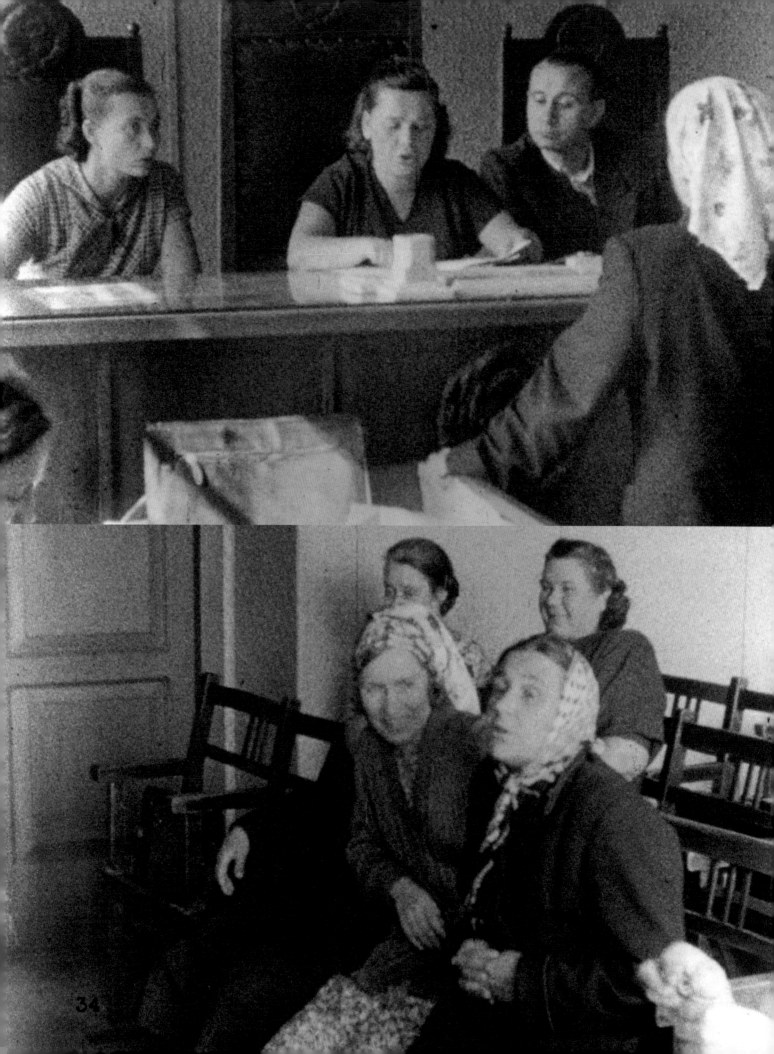

THE NEW SCHOOL ASSOCIATES present

An intimate film report and talk on Russia

1. Russian Closeup

2. Mental Health in Russia

Dr. Karl Men
"I am deli
by Albert Ma

Senator Willi
"I very m
how he was

PLACE: In the New School Auditorium

TIME: On Wednesday, March 25, 1959 — 8:30 p.r

Reservations through Associates' Office
Room 410, 66 West 12th Street
ORegon 5-2700

36

ALBERT MAYSLES

psychologist-cinephotographer recently returned from his

3rd extensive trip

into Soviet Russia

r:

with the film

"

enton:

ike Mr. Maysles' most unusual film . . .
o make it must be an interesting story."

Associate members $1.50
Non-Associates $2.50
Students $1.00

37

ПАВЛОВ
И. П.
1849 - 1936

No Psychoanalysis Found in Russia by Hub Man

By LEO SHAPIRO

The psychiatrist's couch may be a familiar symbol in this country, but in Russia the couch and the psychoanalytical technique are relatively unknown.

So says Albert Maysles of Brookline, 28-year-old instructor in psychology at Simmons College, who visited that country recently with the principal objective of inspecting mental hospitals.

"They don't believe in psychoanalysis. They seem to emphasize the value of rest alone to restore strength to the nervous system. And they claim it's successful. They try to approach the problem of mental health more from a physiological point of view," he indicates.

Maysles expresses surprise that while political prisoners are treated severely, a special kind of sympathetic consideration is given people who are dependent.

"There is no mass treatment of patients in the mental hospitals. The physicians speak in terms of particular diagnoses and treatments for the individual patients as individual cases.

"They have plenty of help. They don't have the bullies you are inclined to get in mental hospitals. And the largest mental hospital in the Soviet Union has only 3000 patients."

Visits Clinic

He looked in on the Korsakow Clinic, a research and teaching hospital which he believes to be Russia's best and which he found to be similar, in some ways, to the Boston Psychopathic Hospital, where he worked on a research project in lobotomy while studying for his master's degree in psychology at Boston University in 1952.

Here he found 30 full-time psychiatrists and 120 psychiatric nurses on hand to look after 140 patients.

He also found Dr. Popov, the head of the clinic, was familiar with the Boston institution, and that all the three hospitals—the others were the Kashchenko and Hospital Region No. 8—there were American journals bearing on the specialty.

"A lot of the methods of treatment were similar to ours. On the other hand, they use electric shock therapy very little. They all regard it as a brutal form of therapy, although some American studies have shown this method to be less injurious to the human brain than the insulin treatment they favor."

Maysles spent parts of 10 days in the Moscow mental hospitals observing their practices.

Waited Week

"All I had with me by way of introduction was five copies of a letter given to me by Dr. Milton Greenblatt, head of research at Boston Psychopathic, an outstanding authority on lobotomy.

"Just before I left for Russia I learned that the Russians, who had used lobotomy in the past, had dropped it in 1951 and outlawed it because they considered it a brutal form of treatment.

"I waited a week before visiting the hospitals and then I showed the letter to an Intourist Service representative who told me visits to hospitals were not part of the service. He was impressed, even though I'm not sure he understood it.

"He called the Ministry of Health and made an appointment for me to see Dr. Babyon, chief of psychiatry of Moscow, who took me to the three hospitals," he says.

He doesn't agree with those who say Russian delegations should not come here because we get nothing in return.

"It's a well known fact that if you want someone to adopt your way of life, you get nowhere just by trying to get them to accept your ideas."

"If they adopt our material way of life, even gradually, the philosophy of democracy is bound to

ALBERT MAYSLES of Brookline, who found that largest mental hospital in Soviet Union had only 3000 patients.

creep in," he observes. He feels strongly that if there is no war their system is going to change and become more like ours.

Stress Peace Need

He says he was asked to stress the need of peace on his return to America because they feel as we do that an atomic war is unthinkable.

"They believe that former President Truman caused the cold war, that we were the aggressors in Korea and Asia and that 'the American people are all right; only the government is bad."

Maysles tells of toasting Boston with Kaganovitch, Malenkov and Mikoyan, of Russia's top leadership, at a function that he crashed.

He recalls a conversation with a Reuters correspondent acting as interpreter, with Malenkov, first Deputy Prime Minister, in the course of which the latter asked him what he was going to do in Russia.

When he replied he planned to visit mental hospitals, he reported Malenkov commented, "We always think there is something wrong with the other person."

The young American educator found great respect among Russians for the contribution this country has made in heart research.

39

MENTALLY ILL RUSSIAN WOMAN GETS FRIENDLY REASSURANCE FROM HOSPITAL PHYSICIAN. MANY SOVIET PSYCHIATRISTS ARE WOMEN

LIFE IN SOVIET MENTAL HOSPITALS

THE STATE medical services of the Soviet Union approach mental health problems from a Pavlovian point of view that differs considerably from the Western approach. Neuroses are generally treated on an ambulatory basis, only severe psychoses are admitted to hospitals. As a result, the mental hospital population is estimated at not more than 100,000.

The attitude of Soviet psychiatrists is based on two main etiologic factors in psychoses: (a) the influence of exterior forces, notably socio-economic factors; (b) the pathophysiologic and metabolic causes of psychoses. The psychoanalytic approach is not practiced because it requires too close a rapport between physician and patient.

Treatment rests heavily on three

methods: electroshock, hypoglycemic shock, and above all sleep therapy. The latter attempts to induce profound "disinhibition" or what has been called "cortical hibernation." Lobotomy and other cerebral surgical procedures were forbidden by law in 1950.

Patients rarely remain more than six months in a mental hospital. If they are not improved by that time they are returned to their families, under supervision; in violent or hopeless cases they are placed in special institutions for chronic psychotics.

The main emphasis of Soviet treatment of mental illness rests on group therapy methods, aimed at restoring the patient's objective links with his environment, or in re-educating so-

cial habits. Even chronic psychotics are organized in social groups, with their own workshops where they can earn a few kopeks. Epileptics have their own "cooperatives" where they can help one another with their problems.

Meanwhile research centers are concentrating on the possible pathophysiologic causes of mental disease, notably on the search for a virus that might cause schizophrenia. The general proportion of psychotics in a Soviet mental hospital is schizophrenics, 30 per cent, arteriosclerotic psychoses, 20 per cent, alcoholic psychoses, 15 per cent.

American psychologist Albert Maysles recently visited several Soviet mental institutions, brought back these exclusive photographs.

PHOTOGRAPHED BY ALBERT MAYSLES

CONTINUED

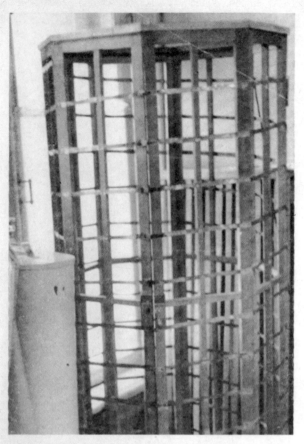

ALCOHOLIC patient is put into a hypnotic trance in an Odessa hospital. Hypnosis is standard procedure.

SUGGESTION THERAPY: patient stands in contraption while a small electric field flows all around him.

PAVLOVIAN conditioning is done on patient (in window) by Prof. Khilchenko at Kiev Pavlov Psychiatric Institute.

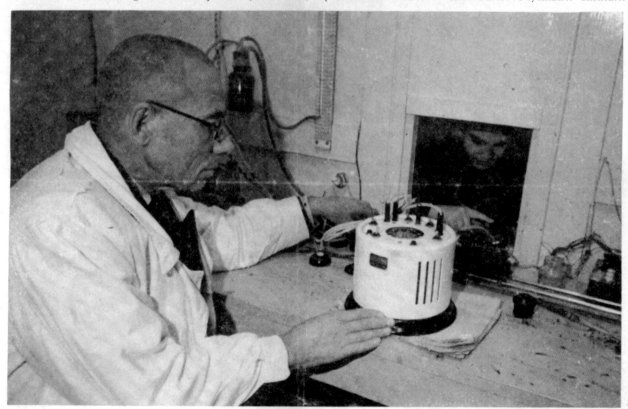

DISTURBED PATIENT IS CARTED OFF BY HOSPITAL ATTENDANTS. HE WILL RECEIVE COURSE OF STANDARD TRANQUILIZING DRUGS

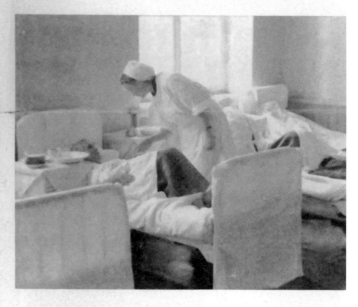

WORK THERAPY is provided wherever possible. Patients in a Moscow hospital (above) are making frames. Emotionally disturbed children (below) are taught biology.

TYPICAL WARD in a Soviet mental hospital is seen above. Below, a patient is given a tranquilizer preparatory to sleep therapy, a favorite Soviet method of treatment.

CONTINUED

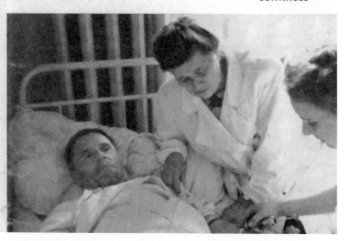

YOUNG PATIENT talks over problems with psychiatrist in Pavlov Institute in Kiev. Psychoanalysis is not used.

SOVIET psychiatry places heavier emphasis on outpatient treatment of less severe mental illnesses, shown below.

GROUP OF PATIENTS at the Kiev mental hospital gather in institution gardens with a psychiatrist and an attendant.

BUST OF PAVLOV perches above psychologist Maysles (with cameras) and group of patients and psychiatrists in Kiev institution.

PATIENT in center is asking interpreter to tell psychologist Maysles that he is satisfied with care in hospital.

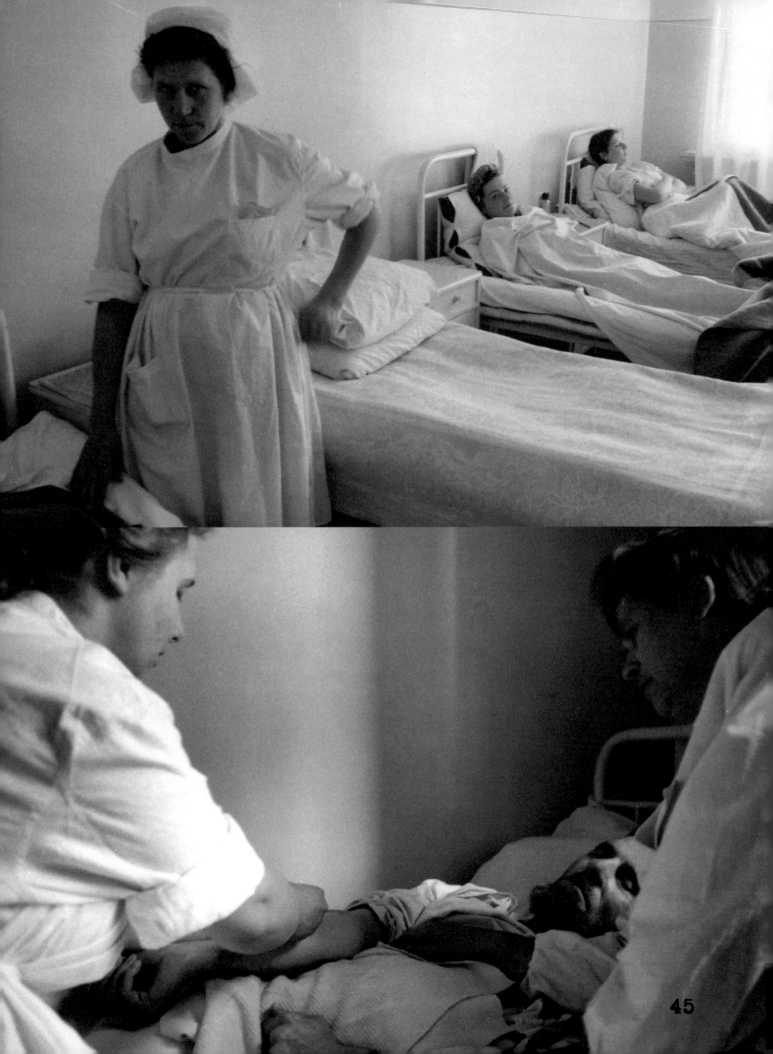

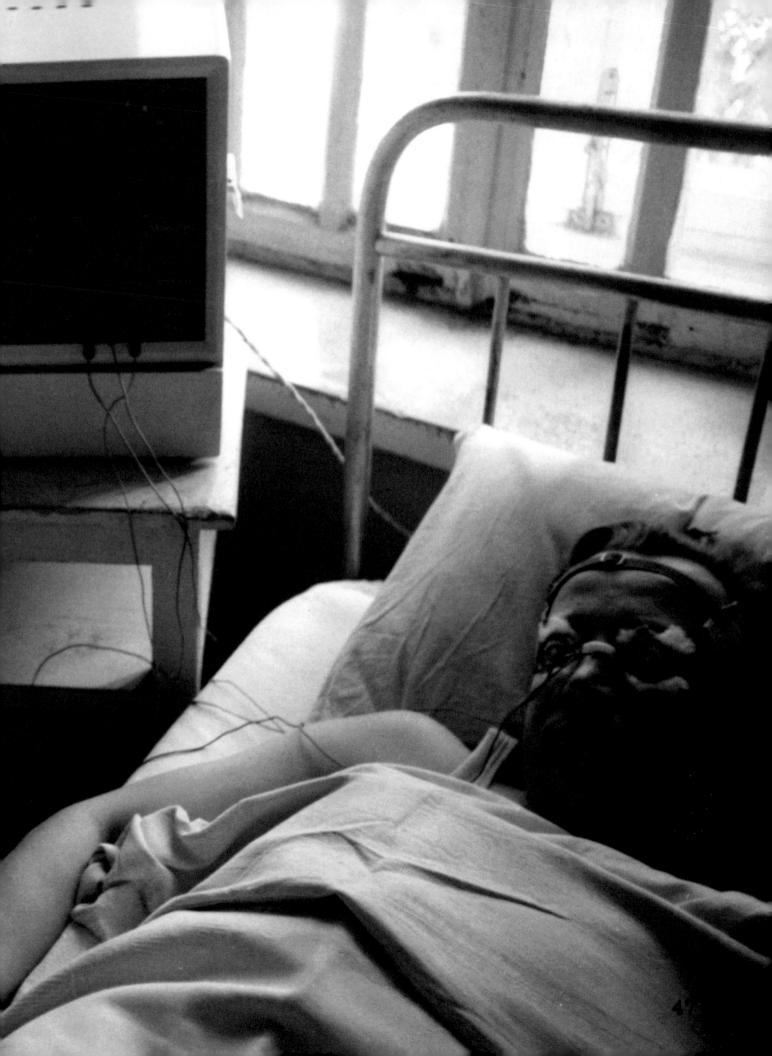

48

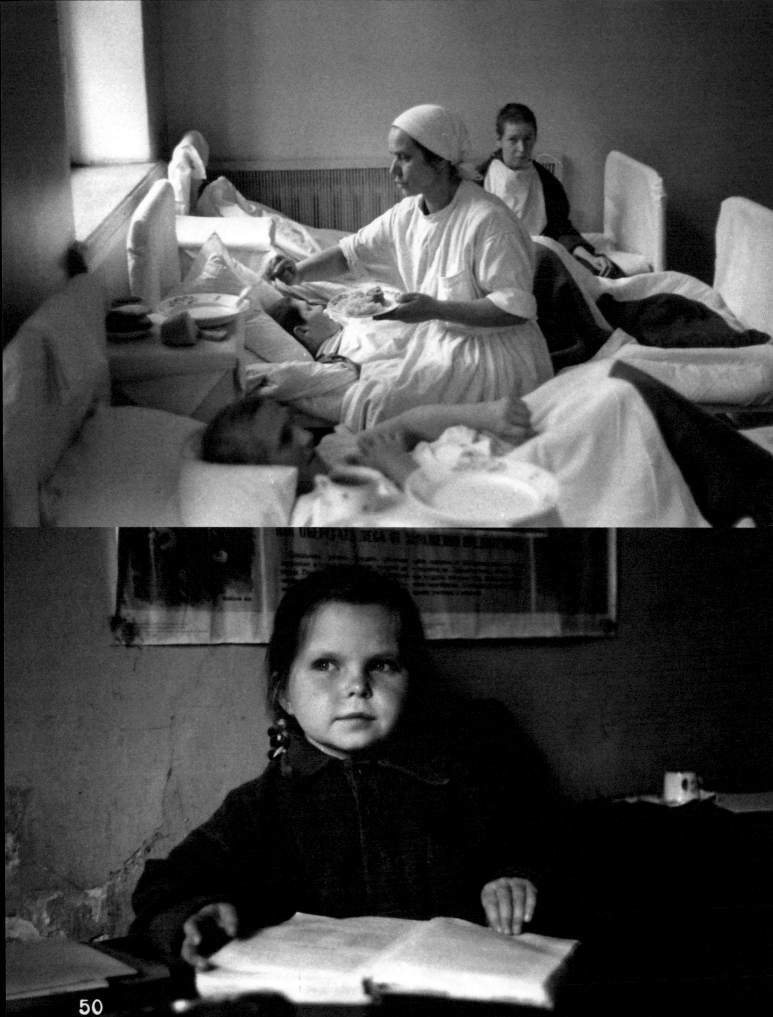

← STUDENTS BRAVING POLISH POLICE

Outside Warsaw's Polytechnic institute, where a year before students had rallied to the support of Wladyslaw Gomulka, Polish students shouted "Gestapo!" "Fascists!" and "Swine!" at the Gomulka police. Inside, 2,000 other students held a protest meeting. The Gomulka government had liquidated the anti-Stalinist weekly, *Po Prostu*, which helped to bring Gomulka to power. Its order triggered Poland's worst riots since the Poznan uprising of June 1956. Thousands of students battled with police for two nights, and hoodlums clashed with them for three more nights. Then fear of Russian intervention and the strong arms of the police brought the situation under control.

65

66

turkey 1958

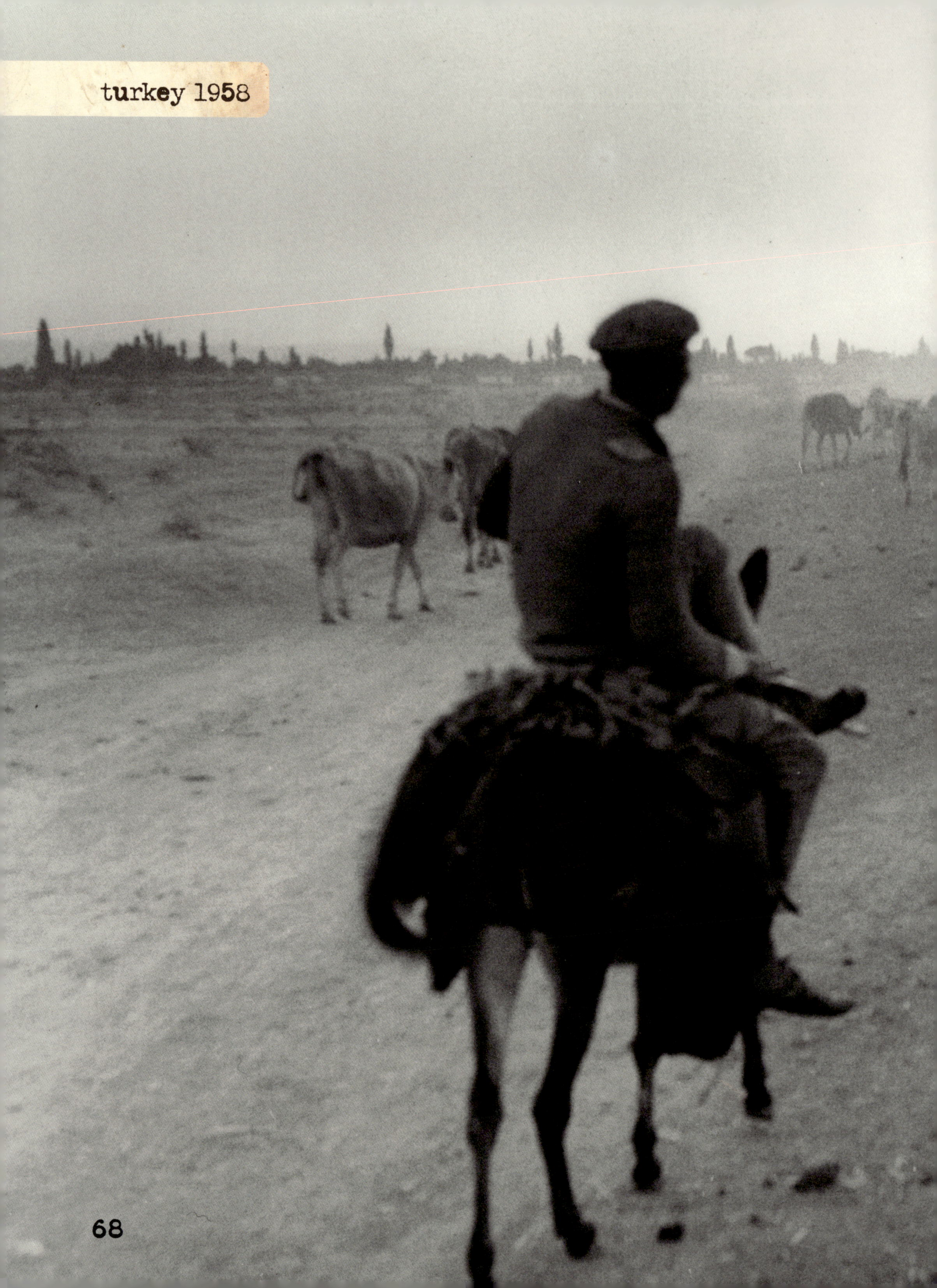

Istanbul Hilton

CABLE: HILTELS ISTANBUL
TELEPHONE: 483200

ISTANBUL · TURKEY

(1st letter from ol' TURKey)

Dear Dad,

Faaaaboooolus!

this place is so great. Wait til you see pictures of the room!

arrived 8^{30} last night and came directly to the room – the greatest! Pateo, the works.

charlie arrived from Rome about ½ hour after me.

I told him about the tentative Roosevelt plans and we are making our schedule on the basis that I might go to Russia with her. ~~So plan~~ naturally, I'd like to hear from you as soon as you find out one way or the other on it.

Had some time to browse around last night and dropped into the biggest belly-dance joint – the Blue Wagon. Fair.

No other news. Must get final tests made on movie camera.

all is O.K. no trouble on customs, or anything. What's new?

Take care.

Love,

al

72

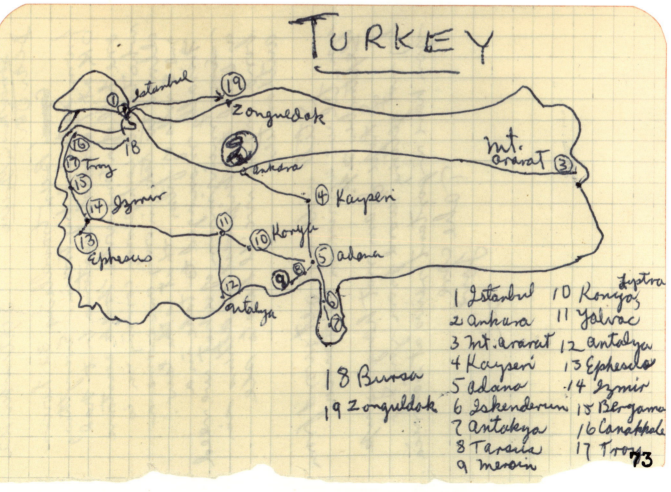

TURKEY

1 Istanbul   10 Konya
2 Ankara   11 Yalvac   Lystra
3 Mt. ararat 12 antalya
4 Kayseri   13 Ephesus
5 adana   14 Izmir
6 Iskenderun 15 Bergama
7 antakya   16 Canakkale
8 Tarsus   17 Troy
9 mersin

18 Bursa
19 Zonguldak

BALIKESIR

ESKISEHIR

ES

modern
PHOTOGRAPHY
F

CONTINUITY...THE KEY TO TRAVEL FILMS

Charles Dee Sharp and Albert Maysles went to the Near East to film the life of St. Paul. The result is a motion picture that not only captures the flavor of the countries they visited, but departs from the standard travel film format. Their approach can be applied by any film maker. Excerpts in color from the script illustrate the film's continuity. Explanations with them will guide you in your own film making.—The Editors

MOST TRAVEL FILMS—amatuer or professional—are great audience chasers. Usually they are boring; occasionally—truly depressing. Main reason? Travel films often are composed of scenes that seem to have been gathered on the same reel purely by accident without any thought of relationship of one shot to another.

We decided that such film was not going to be made by us. And more important, while we planned to shoot a film whose background would be the Near East, we were not going to end up with as trivial a business as most travelogues. First, *Today In The Path of Paul* would attempt to tell something of the journey of St. Paul through the Mediterranean country—the privations he might have suffered, how he lived. Second, the film would tell something about the nature of the countries he visited. But this would not be a costume picture. I was not interested in filming a dramatization of St. Paul's life with actors in flowing robes walking through the Arizona deserts. Many such films had already been made.

While much of the things Paul saw are long gone from the earth, many of the old ruins are still extant—off the beaten path of tourists and so inaccessible few scholars have seen them. *(Continued on page 107)*

"On this road leading to Damascus, Saul of Tarsus . . . was converted . . ."

The opening long shot of the road cuts to the ruins of the pillars, and establishes the idea of the ancient story of Paul. Exposure for the contrasty pillar shot was 24 fps. at f/11. Reading taken with reflected light meter. Because of the extremely strong light of the Mediterranean countries, meter readings had to be taken often and with extreme care.

98

russia 1959

96

97

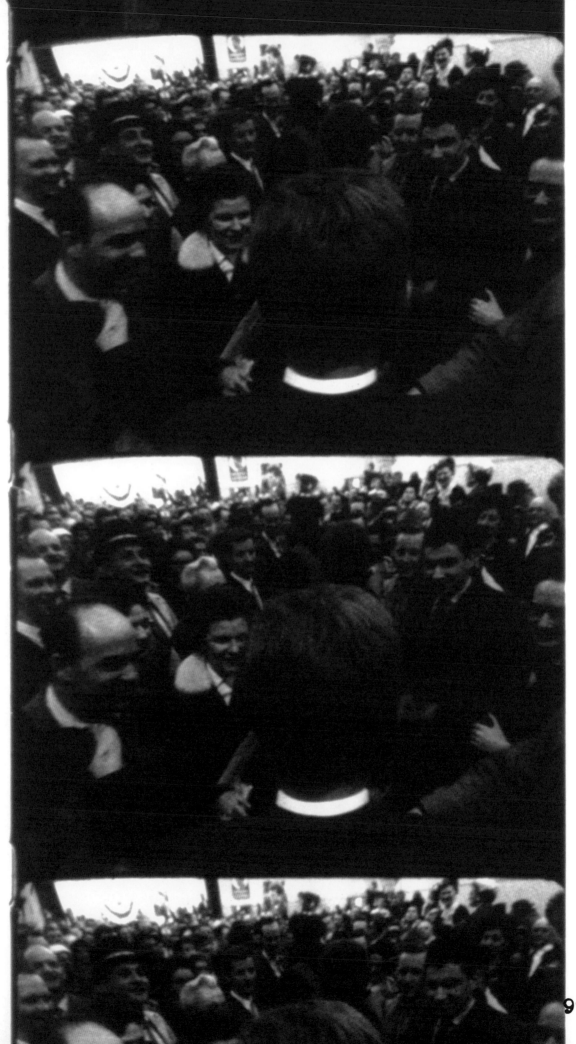

99

100

101

Un fotograma de "Yanquis, No", de Maysles, Leacock y Pennebaker; una película sobre el descontento creciente de los pueblos latinoamericanos contra el imperialismo del Norte en que la Revolución Cubana ocupa un lugar principal.

"YANQUIS, NO"

UNA PELICULA AMERICANA FAVORABLE A CUBA

Entrevista con su autor

HACE varios meses llegó a La Habana un americano con innumerables cámaras, lentes, grabadoras portátiles, micrófonos, etc. Todo cargado y manejado a la vez por él mismo como si fuera una especie de "hombre-orquesta" cinematográfico. Su propósito era registrar cinematográficamente la gran concentración de la Asamblea Popular en la Plaza Cívica. También venía con la intención de captar algunos otros aspectos importantes del hecho revolucionario cubano. Albert Maysles, que este es su nombre, trabajó incansablemente durante varios días y se llevó, al fin, todo el material rodado para incluirlo en una película de una hora sobre la actitud de creciente repulsa de los pueblos latinoamericanos contra el imperialismo. El film en cuestión había de llamarse "Yanquis, no", y hay que reconocer que ninguno de los que estuvimos cerca de su elaboración, estábamos muy seguros (dado el precedente de mala fe de otros periodistas, fotógrafos y reporteros americanos) del uso que se le iba a dar a este material fílmico una vez en los Estados Unidos. Pero las dudas parecen haberse disipado: "Yanquis, no", según todas las referencias que tenemos, ha resultado extremadamente objetiva y, por lo tanto, favorable a la Revolución y ha servido para abrir los ojos a muchos que tuvieron la oportunidad de verla. Por de pronto, las más grandes cadenas de televisión de Estados Unidos se negaron a exhibirla (CBS y NBC), y el periodista Dubois ha comenzado haciendo declaraciones en contra del film que son toda una recomendación. Dice Jules Dubois en un artículo, que la película es "partidarista y desbalanceada"; que, aunque es cierto, como se ve en el film, que hay en la América Latina resentimiento contra los Estados Unidos, este resentimiento "ha sido incitado por los comu-

nistas". Dubois, por fin, acusa también a Worthy, uno de los colabo dores de "Yanquis, no" por haber desafiado al Departamento de Es al hacer un viaje a la China. "Pony" Varona y otros cubanos contrarr lucionarios de allí se han apresurado, por su parte, a hacer declaraci inflamadas contra el film y para terminar, el mismo Raúl Roa se ha trado extremadamente complacido y ha destacado el hecho de que el mostrase a Fidel, no ya como un líder de Cuba, sino de toda la Amé Latina.

Por desgracia, Maysles en su reciente viaje a La Habana, no traer su película para que la viésemos. Habíamos visto, en cambio, anterioridad otra extraordinaria película suya: "Primary", que res cinematográficamente hablando, una pequeña obra maestra. (A Ca Bresson y Elia Kazan se lo pareció también.) Como la técnica que Maysles (que pertenece al grupo de los "Filmakers" junto a Penneb y Leacock) es la última palabra en el género documental decidimos cerle esta entrevista:

—¿En qué consiste, fundamentalmente, su método?

—Nuestro método es el de la objetividad. Vamos a los lugares la cámara y recogemos las imágenes y el sonido tal como son. Desp al editar la película, no añadimos narración, ni forzamos al especta a aceptar nuestra opinión. El mismo debe sacar sus propias conclusi al igual que se hace cuando se conoce algo directamente. Lo importa es no asumir que la cámara va a ser un impedimento, como piensa corr temente. No habrá que prever demasiado las cosas, es mejor ir recog dolas con la cámara a medida que vayan ocurriendo. En "Yanquis, seguimos este método objetivo y sin propaganda. Es por esto que ha aceptada y le ha gustado hasta a la gente en mi país que antes esta en contra de Castro por prejuicio e ignorancia. Nuestra película mue la realidad con tal evidencia que al espectador no le queda más reme que aceptarla.

Maysles continúa su tema con entusiasmo:

—En contra de lo que es aceptado, yo creo que el verdadero cine por hacer. Tengo la impresión de que, en realidad, se ha rozado solame la superficie del cine. Creo que se está comenzando ahora y que por empieza a vislumbrarse la oportunidad de hacer grandes films. Com he dicho, todo consiste en no forzar nada de la realidad con la cám dejar hacer a la naturaleza, enseñar las cosas tal como son... Lo extra

El joven camarógrafo-director Albert Maysles fil-mando en nuestra Plaza Cívica con su pequeño equi-po portátil con sonido sincronizado.

TELEVISION
Two Men & a Camera

The pretty, excited girl might have been chanting "We want a touchdown." But she was yelling something else, and for a moment the meaning did not register. Then it did, with a shock: *"Cuba, si; Yanki, no!"*

The girl was one of a mass of Cubans who crowded into Havana's Plaza Civica last summer to cheer Fidel Castro and shout hatred of the U.S. Hers was one of many memorable faces—faces of hate, sorrow, bewilderment—that dominated a new, hour-long documentary seen on ABC-TV last week. Billed as a "film editorial," it was designed to give viewers a look at the dangerous anti-American passions mounting throughout Latin America in the vacuum of U.S. policy.

The hour-long show had a rough-and-ready air about it. Frequently the sound was so bad that words were indistinguishable. Some of the camera work was shaky, some of the cutting rough. As an editorial, the program was impassioned rather than closely reasoned. But the report hit like a fist and left some haunting images in the viewers' minds: the despair of an out-of-work electrician's helper in a dirt-floored hut in Caracas; the satisfaction of a fisherman whose family has a fine new cottage in a Cuban cooperative—and the naively shrewd question of an old crone about how the family's wretched old furniture would look in the new house.

The documentary, first of a prospective series of six to be produced by TIME INC. and ABC-TV, is the work of Producer Robert Drew, 36, a former jet pilot and LIFE correspondent. His technique of candid-camera closeups and of eliminating an on-screen commentator is not new, but he uses it more deliberately and effectively than any TV show has before. Drew employs two-man crews (one man handles camera, one sound, and both also act as reporters and editors) instead of the usual unwieldy task force. Says Drew: "We would not move in with our lights and cameras and convert a worker's shack into a television studio. That way you simply don't get a feeling of reality." Using natural lighting, a stripped-down 16-mm. camera and, if necessary, a midget recording machine, Drew's reporting teams do their work unobtrusively, spend as long as a week befriending a family till they are willing to talk freely.

TV critics almost unanimously applauded the show. If Producer Drew's technique is obviously not applicable to all themes, *Yanki, No!* is an exciting start in a series that promises to use pictures, rather than what Drew calls "word logic," in bringing TV closer to reality.

MOVIES ABROAD
Visual De Tocqueville

"Before such an extraordinary document," wrote the Communist *Lettres Françaises* grudgingly, "one can't help admiring the candor with which Americans portray their army. The fact that a French producer was authorized to make such a film indicates great liberalism." The film is a 24-minute short titled *The Marines*, and its producer is François Reichenbach, 38, who made a big New Wave splash last spring with his first full-length movie, the much criticized *L'Amérique Insolite* (generally translated "unusual"). For his latest effort, a stark study of the Parris Island, S.C., boot camp, Reichenbach last week was unanimously greeted as one of France's most poetic, powerful film makers.

MOVIEMAKER REICHENBACH
From beats to boots.

Starting with slope-shouldered, checker-shirted young boys "not knowing what to do with their bodies or souls," *The Marines*, in a series of vivid, violent images and startling closeups, follows the grim process of making men of them. Naked torsos are lined up in a sterile examination room like sheep. Barbers briskly shear them. Then come the relentless weeks of screamed orders and merciless reprimands ("Hey, stupid, you shave this morning?" "Get that crummy chin up!"), reaching a crescendo in the savagery of bayonet drill. "Downward slash!" barks the drillmaster. "You know what that means." At that point, the Paris audience invariably gasps.

"*The Marines*," commented French Director Roger Vadim (who gave the world Brigitte Bardot), "plants a sword in the human consciousness, for it tells of young volunteers who, in order to prove their human identity, accept precisely the contrary: loss of their individuality . . . Still, I know well while writing these words freely that I owe my freedom in part to other shaved-headed young men who 16 years ago brandished these bayonets on beaches now boasting bloody names."

Love at First Sight. One of Reichenbach's most successful efforts is his musical score; *The Marines* opens with rock 'n' roll, drowns out roaring sergeants with soaring cellos, beats jungle drums during bayonet drill, concludes with Beethoven's *Grand Fugue*. That kind of startling contrast has become the trademark of the many-talented, Paris-born moviemaker whose first creative work was collaborating on songs, some of them for Edith Piaf. In 1947 he visited the U.S., fell "crazy in love with that country," stayed on for five years as a consultant to art museums.

Not until 1953, when he bought a tiny, wrist-strapped, 16-mm. camera to film the Grand Prix de Paris, did Reichenbach find his calling, and begin to make short documentaries about the U.S. For

"YANKI, NO!": CUBAN MILITIAMEN
Beyond word logic.

104

105

109

111

112

115

117

118

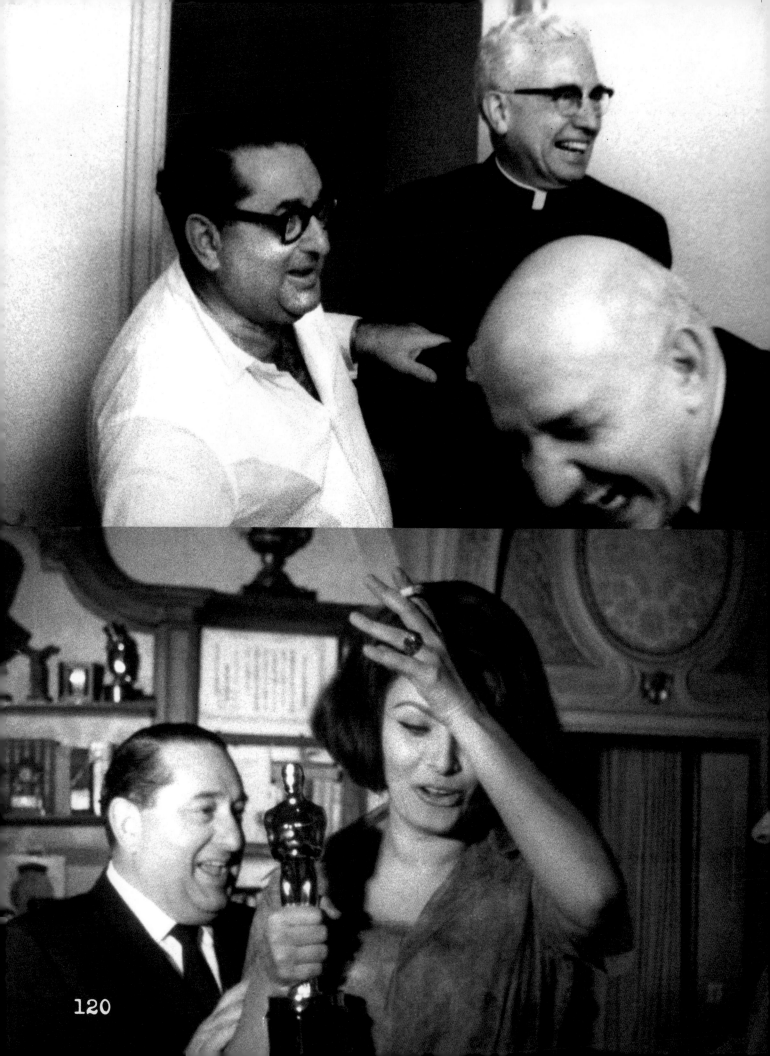

123

125

128

129

WHAT'S HAPPENING!

THE BEATLES IN THE U.S.A.

WHAT'S HAPPENING!

THE BEATLES IN THE U.S.A.

WHAT'S HAPPENING!

133

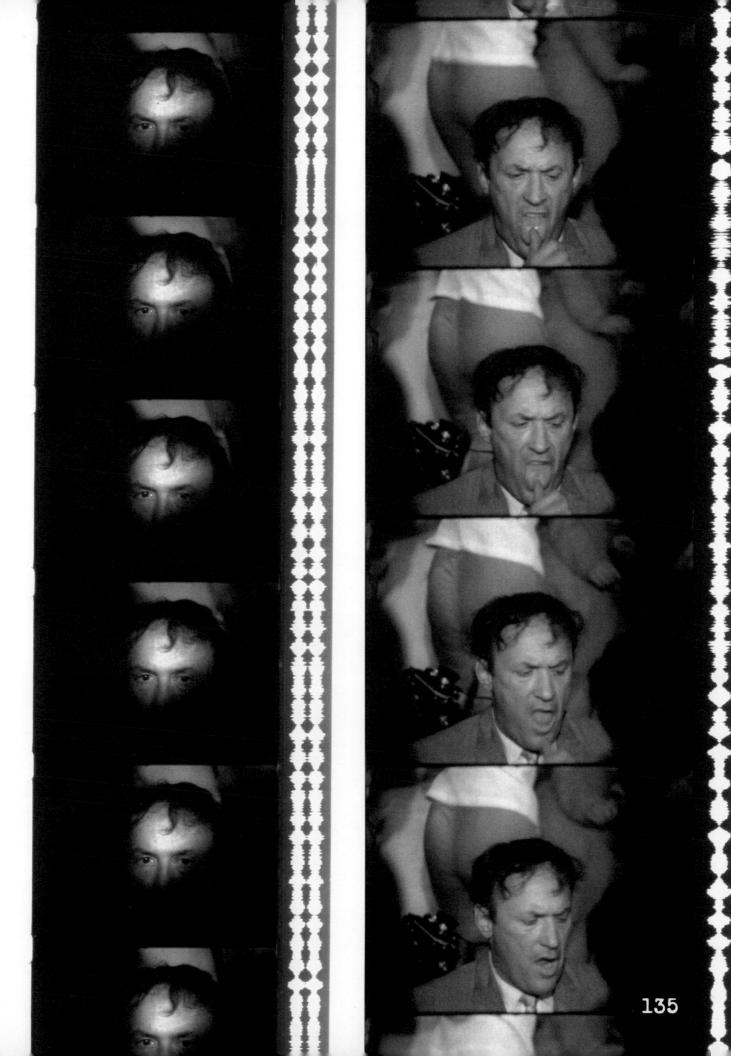

135

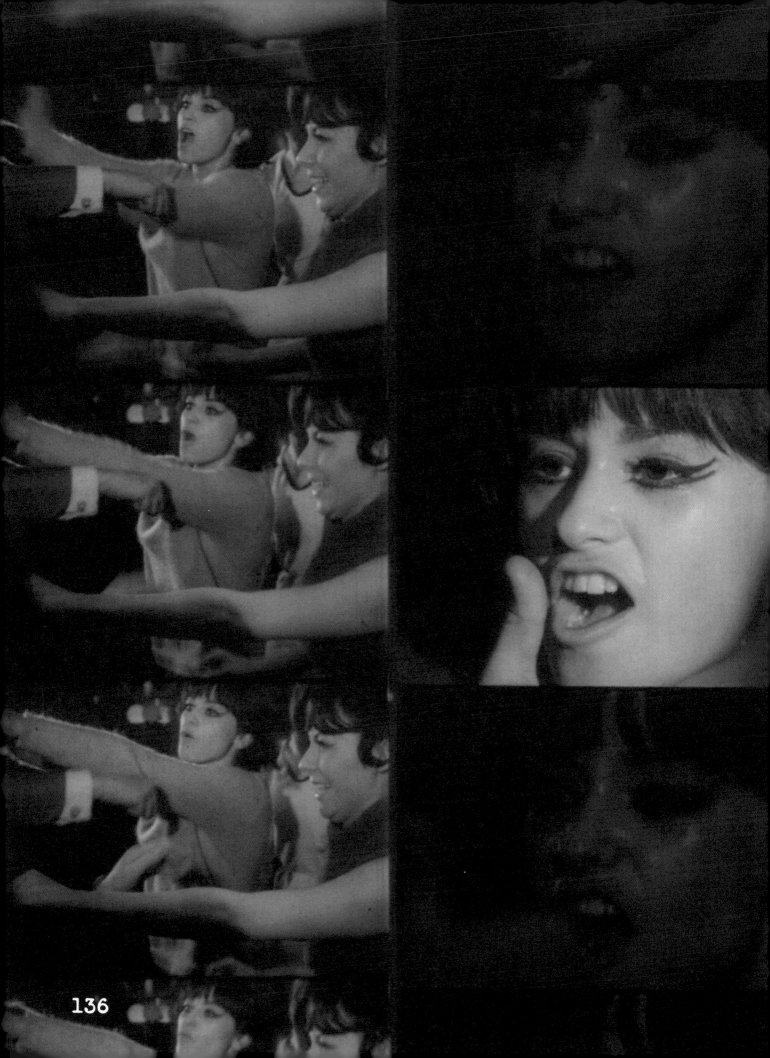

137

WE'RE HAVING LUNCH TODAY WITH MARLON BRANDO, FOLKS

It's like they always say— people don't really communicate anymore

To hawk *Morituri, a well-meaning, fast-moving flick, they brought Marlon Brando cast, and from miles around they came to stare and wonder. A movie star, one of the wildest, captured and tamed! On one particular day they sat him down in New York's Hampshire House and hour after hour fed him an endless stream of television interviewers. They also gave him lunch and several drinks. How did he react to all these stimulants? The answer has been filmed for posterity by David and Albert Maysles who hope to exhibit it on television. These pages are a sampler: don't miss the whole thing when it comes to your neighborhood living room, for God's sake — you won't know how to proceed with your life.*

LOIS LEPPART, KMSP-TV, Minneapolis: Marlon Brando *(sighing)*, one of the most exciting and talented men in America today . . .

BRANDO: Oh, come on!

LEPPART *(laughing)*: . . . and certainly, if I may make a pun, please. Physically and mentally you are now not an "ugly American." You're anything but. But certainly, physically, there's so much activity in all of the movies that. . . .

BRANDO: When was the last time you saw me nude? *(Laughter.)*

LEPPART: I suppose we have to talk about *Morituri*. It's a . . .

BRANDO: Let's not. Do we have to?

LEPPART: It's a wonderful show.

BRANDO: Did you see it?

LEPPART: No, I haven't seen it yet.

BRANDO: Then how do you know?

LEPPART: Because I've talked to people that previewed it and they tell me that it's very suspenseful.

BRANDO: Now, that's the point . . . we mustn't believe propaganda. It might be an absolutely terrible film —you don't know—we have to make up our own minds about it. I think that's essential. And don't . . . you shouldn't . . . make up your mind about that picture until you see it.

LEPPART: You know this is sort of your whole personality. In a capsule. Not to believe. . . .

BRANDO: How do you know what my personality is?

LEPPART: Because I have met you and you radiate your personality.

BRANDO: Really? *(Laughter.)*

BILL GORDON, KGO-TV, San Francisco: There's a motion picture called *Morituri*—we better get all the plugs in, because Twentieth Century-Fox has spent a zillion bucks.

BRANDO: Now, wait a minute . . . I object.

GORDON: You mean in my relating to Twentieth Century-Fox?

Brando: No—it seems that every time we get in front of this television, everybody starts hustling.

GORDON: Yes.

BRANDO: Well, you feel that you're obliged to hustle the picture and I feel reduced to hucksmanship.

GORDON: But after all, they did pay a fortune for this purpose . . . we would never be sitting here if they didn't want to huckster the picture.

BRANDO: I don't think we ought to sneak around it. I think we ought to say we're here as hucksters.

GORDON: Yes.

BRANDO: He's a newsman and I'm a huckster! And I'm thumping the tub for a picture called *Morituri*.

MARY FRANN, WBKB-TV, Chicago: Mr. Marlon Brando. Very often. . . .

BRANDO: You're one of the pre interviewers that I've met.

FRANN: Thank you. You're one most gracious hosts I've met.

BRANDO *(smiling)*: Oh, really

FRANN: Mr. Brando, very often have been called by members o press uncooperative and. . . .

BRANDO: Uncooperative in wha spect—in relation to what?

FRANN: In making films, with producers and the directors—s times working with you . . we've never really heard your sion. Your side, or what your ings are about this. You s certainly to us today to be a gracious and articulate man.

BRANDO: Well, I don't really t it's worth the candle to go into defense of those spurious acc tions. I think that people us make up their own minds about and . . . it's sort of boring to go such things and an explanatio how you have been chastised o cused or. . . .

FRANN: Well, why has so much written about this in the press

BRANDO: People don't realize th press item—a news item—is mo And that news is hawked in same way that shoes are, toothp or lipstick or hair tonic or anyt else . . . and if you put somethin the paper about Liz Taylor or R ard Burton everybody's going buy it. Everybody wants to k about that. So, it becomes an it A sellable item. The merchandi aspect of the press is not really f recognized, I think, by the pu And . . . when you don't coope with those merchandising syste people that sell news like He Hawker . . . hmmm . . . that's a g mistake! Hedda Hawker. . . .

FRANN: You chose to keep it . . . didn't correct it!

BRANDO: You know, it's sort of unwritten code that if you d cooperate with those people and them all about the intimacies your personal life—then yo broken the rule and you have to publicly chastised for it—or c bically plastised for it, if you b And . . . well, that's the way of world out there. But I've found and large that people make up th own minds.

FRANN: Thank you very much this visit. I certainly am. . . .

BRANDO: Well, I hope this isn't end of our career! *(Laughter.)*

JOHN ANTHONY, WITI-TV, Milwaukee: We have the pleasure n of talking to perhaps one of the most famous actors in the worl Mr. Marlon Brando. . . .

BRANDO: Yes . . . when I get finis with the roast beef.

ANTHONY: (All right. You keep e ing, and I'll keep introducin . . . who has played a variety of ro from Shakespearean in producti like *Julius Caesar* to, of cour Stanley Kowalski in *Streetc Named Desire*. He received Academy Award for *On the Wat front* in 1954—is that correct?

BRANDO: I guess so.

ANTHONY: And the big thing about you, Marlon, is . . .

BRANDO: My stomach.

ANTHONY: How do you account for this very great versatility? Is it something you studied or does it just come to you naturally?

BRANDO: Ah . . . I don't know, you can say the same thing about a hula hoop. It catches on and everybody buys it, and it's quite popular for a while, and then disappears, like fly-swatters.

ANTHONY: Umhummm.

BRANDO: Hardly anybody buys a fly-swatter nowadays.

ANTHONY: Well, the point of the question was . . . basically I think we should talk about *Morituri*.

BILL GORDON: Would you rather not huckster anymore? We haven't seen this picture yet, but I'm here to tell you I'll bet it's a great picture, isn't it, Marlon?

BRANDO: It sure is, pal. No, all the pictures that they make in Hollywood are really great films, and everybody knows that!

GORDON: They haven't made a bad picture there in . . .

BRANDO: . . . in ninety years!

GORDON: That's right. That last picture, *Lassie Gets Bar Mitzvah'd*, that was probably the last bad picture that I think Hollywood made.

BRANDO: Bill, it's been wonderful talking to you and, gee, that's a real checkered coat . . . and . . . Vote for Willkie! (*Laughter*.)

GORDON: Marlon Brando! We'll be right back, after these messages of great interest! (Fade-out—commercial break.)

MICHELE METRINKO, WNAC-TV, Boston: Our viewing audience would like to know why you're here and for you to tell us about your latest movie . . .

BRANDO: How old are you—

METRINKO: . . . *Morituri*.

BRANDO: No, you? Twenty-three?

METRINKO: No, I'll be twenty-one in March.

BRANDO: Twenty-one. . . .

METRINKO: Yes . . . but this is supposed to be a woman's privilege.

BRANDO: What is?

METRINKO: Her age.

BRANDO: You're talking like an American adage.

METRINKO: No, please—do tell us about your new movie!

BRANDO: Well—why?

METRINKO: Because we're looking forward to seeing it in Boston.

BRANDO: That's the thing. Are you?

METRINKO: We certainly are.

BRANDO: Excuse me, I didn't mean to touch your ankle! What can I tell you about it?

METRINKO: Oh, if you'd like to tell us something about, oh, behind the scenes while you were making the picture or. . . .

BRANDO: How far behind the scenes?

METRINKO: Oh, just some interesting things our audience would like to hear about!

BRANDO: Well. . . .

METRINKO: I'm sure you've run into. . . .

BRANDO: Bernie Wicki [the director of *Morituri*] smokes the worst

cigars of anyone I ever knew. (*Laughter*.) I hate his cigars. And . . . he smokes cigars that were made of—they got some shoes from Italian fishermen, with rope soles, rope-soled sandals, they crushed them up and mashed them around and sent them to Vladivostok. (*Publicist hands Brando a note*.) She was Miss U.S.A.! Is that a fact?

METRINKO: Yes, it is.

BRANDO: Well, I . . . I could have guessed!

METRINKO: That's very sweet of you.

BRANDO: Well, you know it's unusual to find somebody as beautiful as you are who is also a college graduate, and seriously interested in world affairs and studying law.

METRINKO: Well, I enjoyed being Miss U.S.A.

BRANDO: She was Miss U.S.A.—what year was that?

METRINKO: In '64.

BRANDO (*to audience*): In 1964 she was Miss U.S.A. I asked her if she was pretty and she said she—well, that was a subjective opinion and she didn't really know.

METRINKO: Well, there were only six judges that decided, so I don't think that's very decisive.

BRANDO: Yes, but you went through several stages to arrive finally at—the title, didn't you?

METRINKO: Yes.

BRANDO: So it was really more than six judges?

METRINKO: Well, six here and six there . . . and I was very honored. But, Mr. Brando! Thank you so much for being our guest.

BRANDO: Good night, folks. Smoke Optimo cigars.

BILL GORDON: Let's talk about contact lenses. I read someplace that you got six new. . . .

BRANDO: You've got the longest fingernails of anybody I've seen.

GORDON: Only on one side. You see I play the classic guitar, so . . .

BRANDO: Oh, really?

GORDON: . . . so you have to have long fingernails on your right hand to play the strings and short fingernails to fret. That's what I do for my kicks. What do you do?

BRANDO: I fret a lot. Does everybody know you play the classic guitar?

GORDON: No. But they do now.

BRANDO: Well, he does play the classical guitar, and if you hold up your fingers on your right hand so they can see it. . . .

GORDON: Well, if you do it that way, it's feminine.

BRANDO: Well, that's all right. Listen, we all have feminine and masculine aspects in our personality. . . .

GORDON: We'll be right back after these messages of great interest. But first — remember Marlon Brando in the Twentieth Century-Fox motion picture, *Morituri*. It's a great picture and he's a great actor.

BRANDO: For God's sake, go see it. You won't really know how to proceed in life if you don't see *Morituri*. It's one of the most important things you'll ever do. ⧻

141

142

143

144

146

149

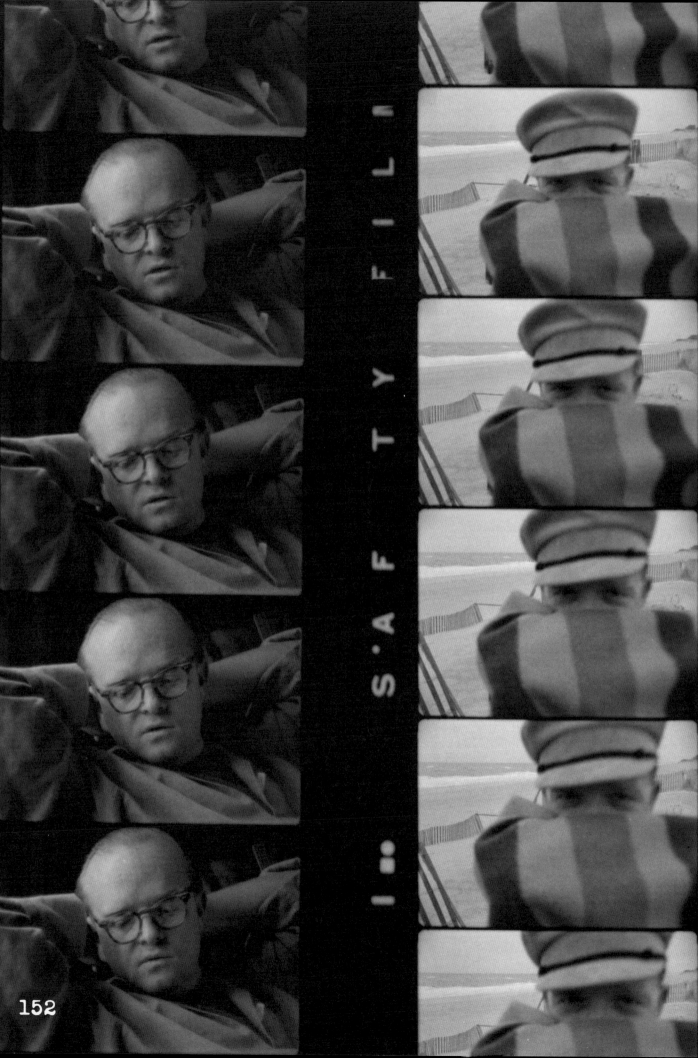

152

153

155

158

157

158

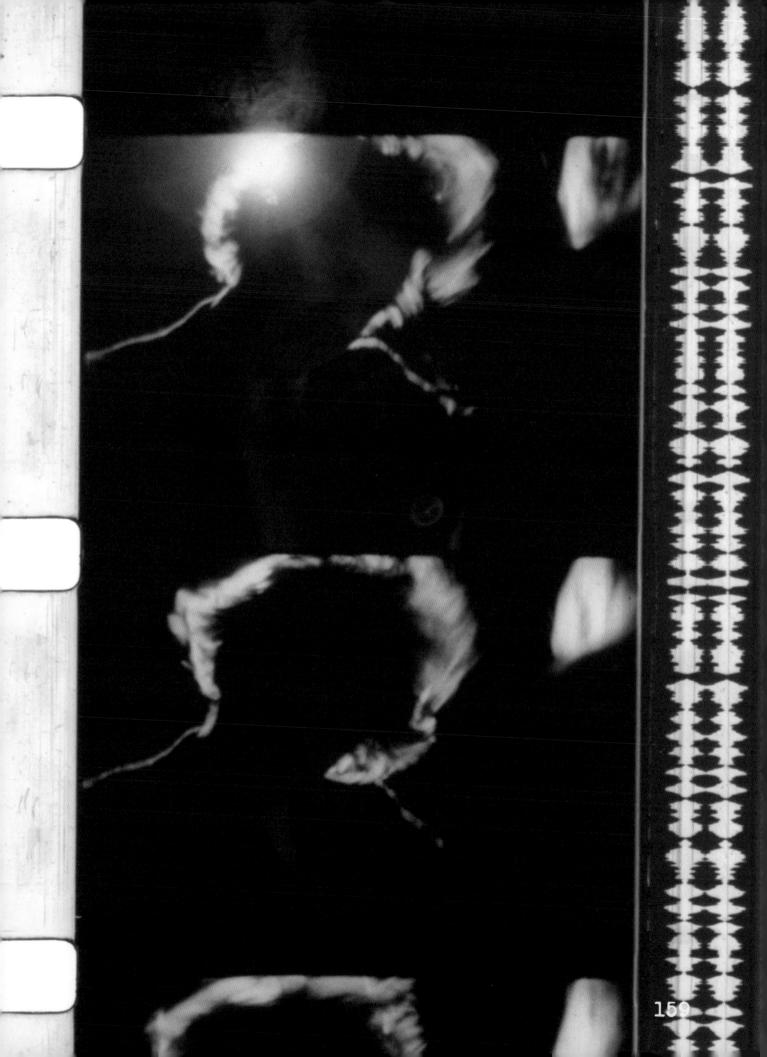

159

161

162

163

164

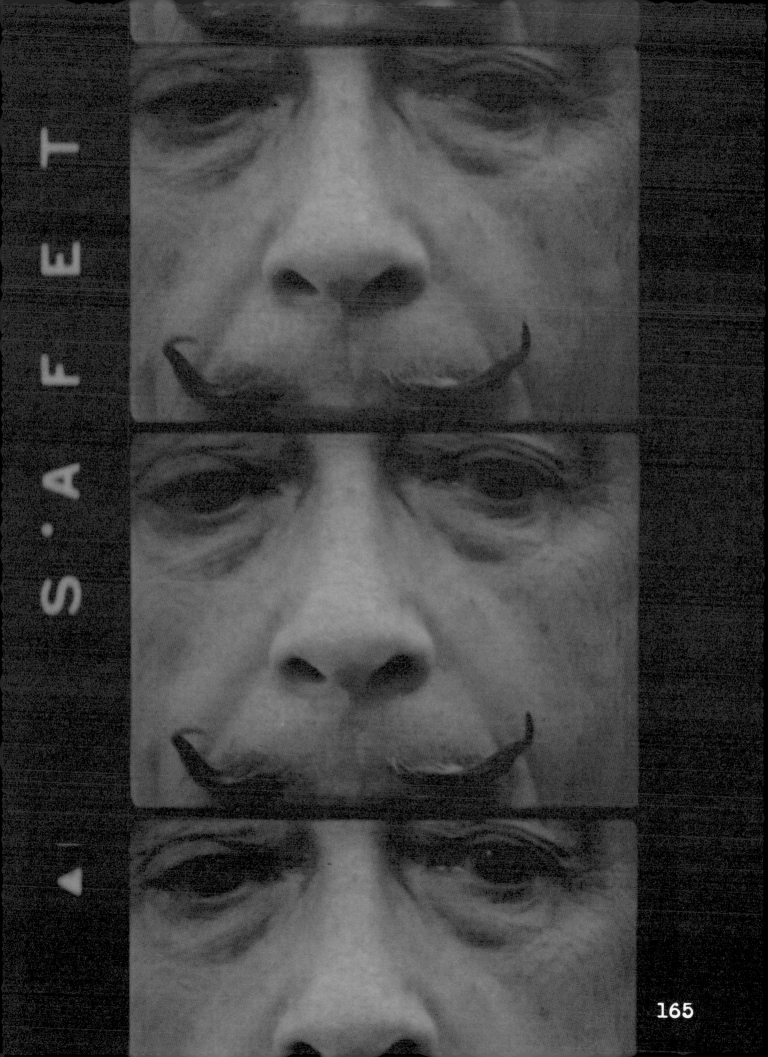

September 9, 1966

The South Western Company
2968 Foster Creighton Drive
Nashville, Tennessee 37211

Attention: Mr. Dortch Oldham

Dear Sirs:

We plan to produce a film about a door-to-door
salesman who fits (as close as possible) the
description of the "Yankee drummer": a dedicated,
top-notch, full-time salesman who sells in a rural
area of the U.S.A. and stays on the road for at
least a few days at a time. The New England states
would be preferred but not absolutely necessary.

We realize that the salesman we've described is
not at all common. However, I think you will agree
with our hunch that at least a few still exist. It
is our goal to find such a man for the film.

Can you recommend a salesman who fits this description?
We would appreciate any help you can give us. Thank
you.

Sincerely,

David C. Maysles

DCM:no

CRITERIA FOR OUR SALESMAN

1. He should be selling FAMILY BIBLE (picture bible for $40-$50)

    non primarily the Catholic Encyclopedia nor magazines or

other premium gimmicks

2. Does he sell with leads or knock on random doors cold? Does he

work alone or with a partner?

3. Where is the territory? We would like it semi-rural or rural.

    New England ideal.

4. How long is he on the road? We prefer at least a few days at

a time.

5. What type of customer does he encounter? Income level? religion?

We would like "straightforward American types"...not Bible belt or

"Southern exotics."

6. Besides being a salesman, what's going on in his life? Family,

friends, activities

7. Should be a full-time salesman--a regular guy not more than 50 years

old.

8. What kind of sales presentation does he make?

9. How does he feel aboutx selling?

10. Most important: He must be a likeable guy, some one you can look

at for over an hour; at least moderately successful in his work.

He must have some depth and be somewhat aware ps of what's going on

around him. This is a dramatic human interest story(with the same

criteria as a feature film), not in xx any way an "information film"

or an expose.

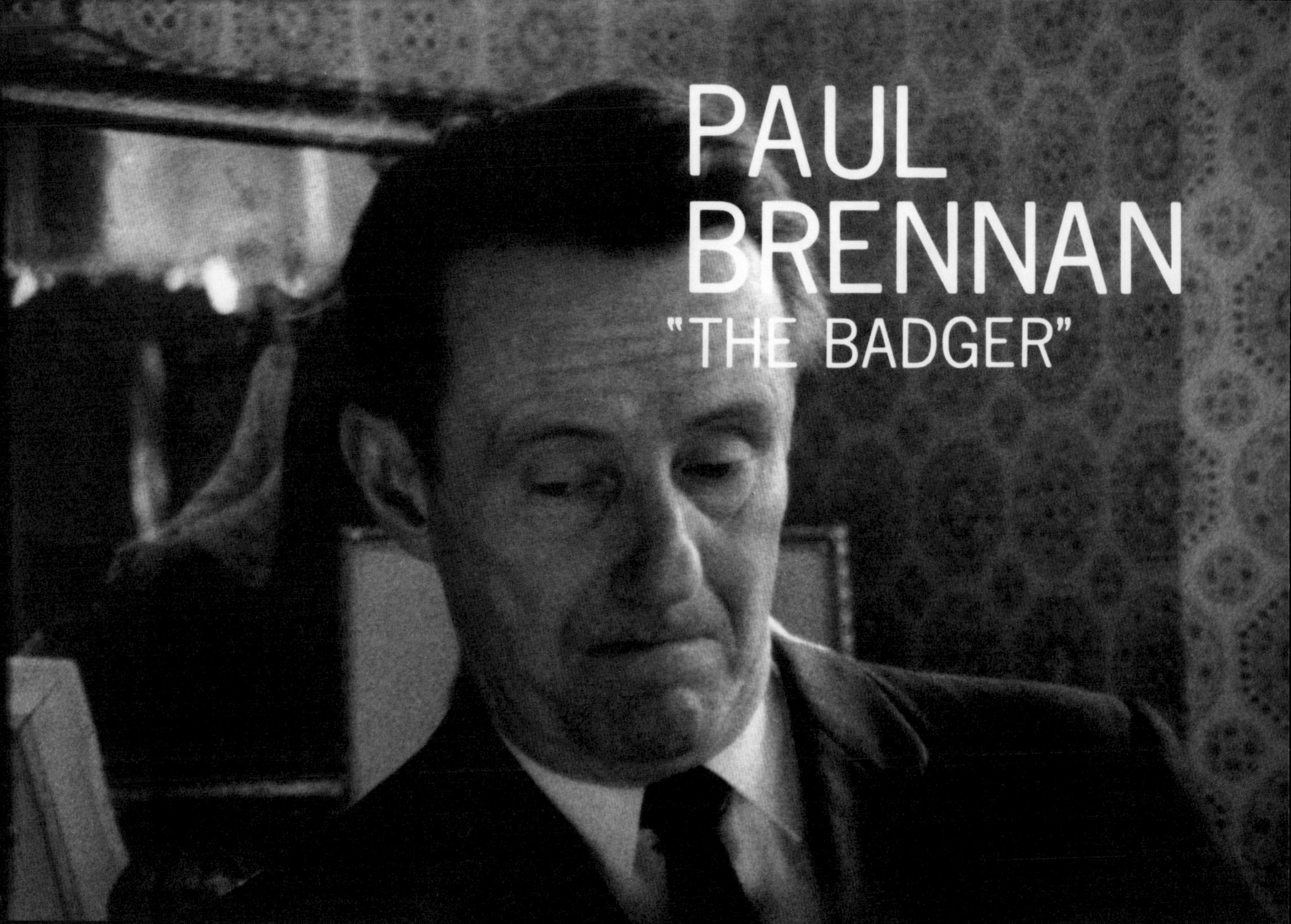

PAUL
BRENNAN
"THE BADGER"

JAMES
BAKER
"THE RABBIT"

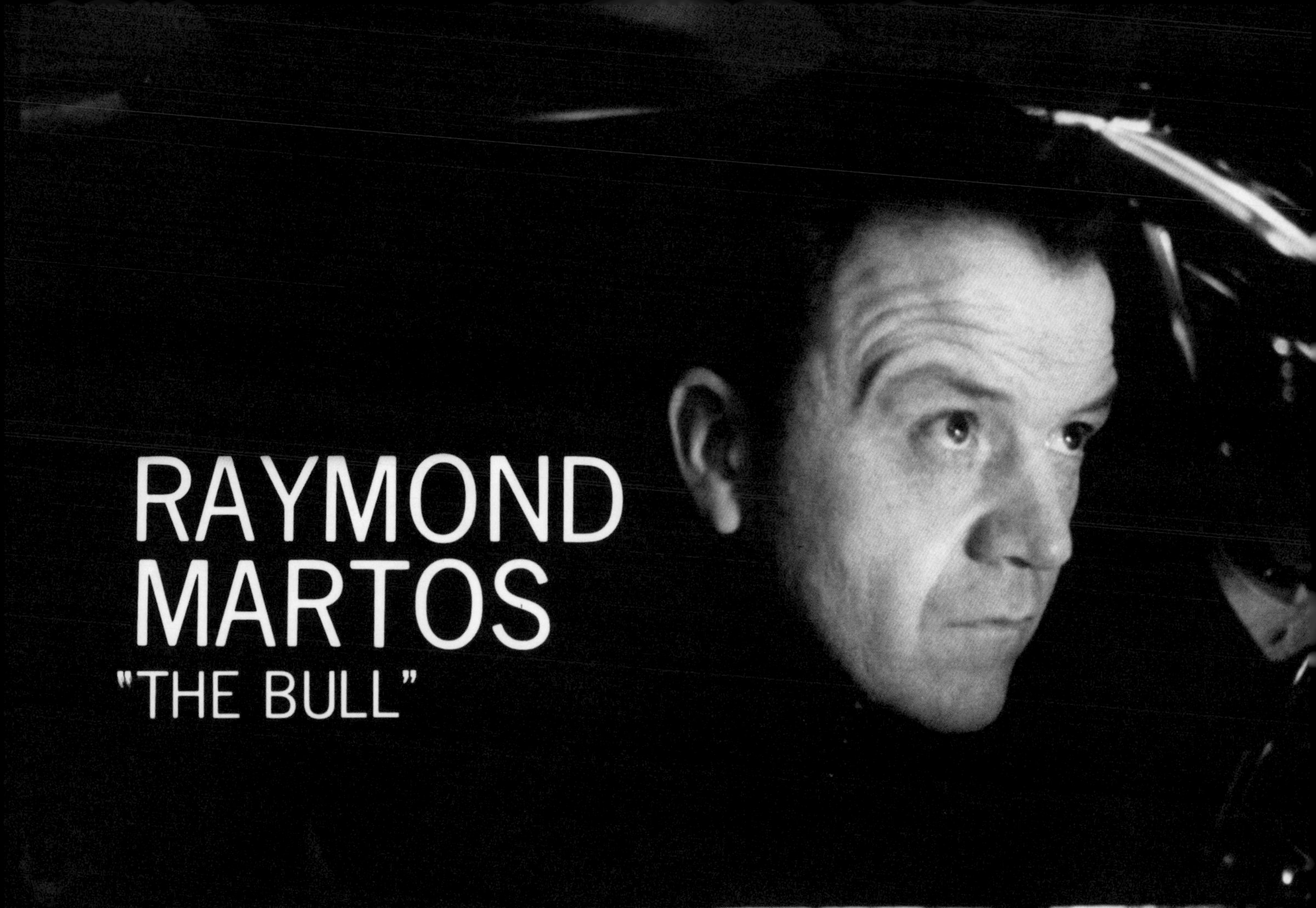

RAYMOND
MARTOS
"THE BULL"

CHARLES
MC DEVITT
"THE GIPPER"

172

174

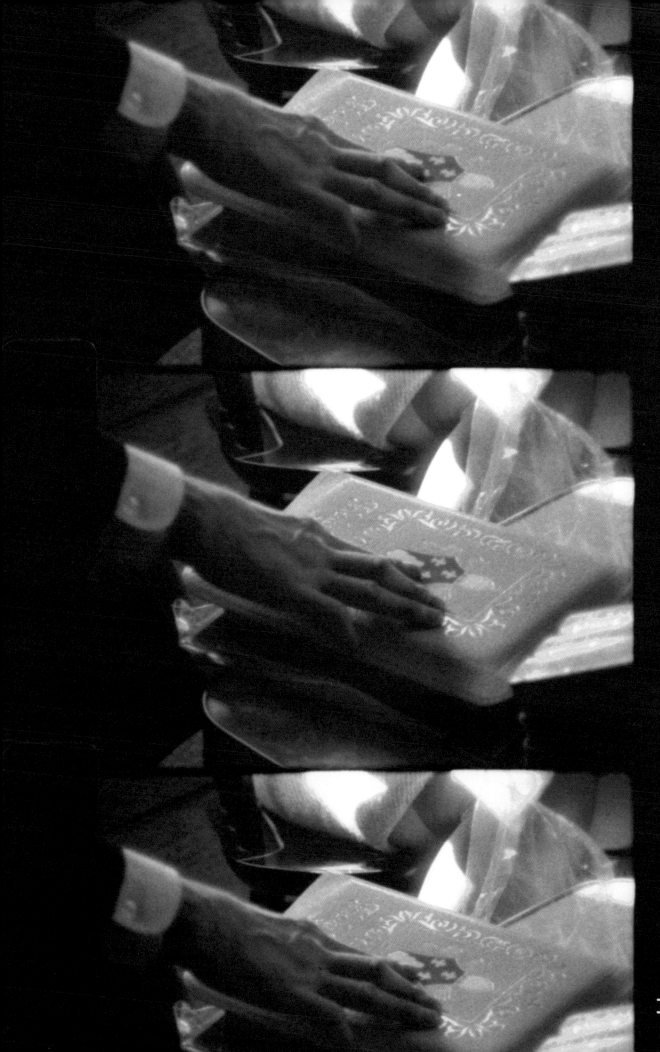

177

181

184

18

"I was spellbound.

A beautiful film. I've seen SALESMAN three times and each time I've been more impressed. A cinematic mural of faces, words, motel rooms, parlors and streets. As strange and exotic a journey as any. Fascinating, comic, poignant, very funny."

—Vincent Canby, New York Times

THE MAYSLES BROTHERS'

SALESMAN

A FILM BY THE MAYSLES BROTHERS AND CHARLOTTE ZWERIN

68th St. PLAYHOUSE
3rd Avenue at 68th St. · RE 4-0302
1·00 2·40 4·50 6·05 7·50 9·35 11·15

189

"As strange and exotic a journey as any. Fascinating, comic, poignant, very funny. A beautiful film."
—Vincent Canby, New York Times

SALESMAN

3rd Avenue at 68th St.
RE 4-0302

68th St. PLAYHOUSE

1:20, 3, 4:40,
6:25, 8:10, 9:55

SAT. ONLY   1, 2:35, 4:15, 6,
                   7:45, 9:30, 11:15

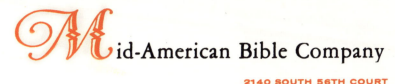 **Mid-American Bible Company**

2140 SOUTH 56TH COURT   CHICAGO, ILLINOIS 60650
AREA CODE 312   PHONE 656-4800

EV. THOMAS B. McDONOUGH
S.T.L., J. D.
Theological Consultant

OFFICERS AND DIRECTORS

ARGROVE E. TURNER
President

ENNIE M. TURNER
Vice President

ONALD N. JENKINS
Vice President

BIN P. TURNER
Sec'y. Treas.

January 3, 1969

Mr. D. Porter Bibb, III
Maysles Films, Inc.
1697 Broadway
New York, New York 10019

Dear Mr. Bibb:

Congratulations on

an unusually good presentation with deep
understanding of the good and bad in salesmanship.

Your picture, THE SALESMAN, includes a fine character
study of the kind of man who looks great to every sales
manager during an interview, but really shouldn't be
hired at all in the first place.

Many emotions are awakened through the fine natural
presentation of your story and whether it is Bibles or
water coolers it becomes obvious to any sales-minded
person, through your story, what a man should not feel
or think in his attempt to become successful.

From an entertainment point of view, housewives should
find much fun in viewing it.

Yours very truly,

MID-AMERICAN BIBLE COMPANY

Hargrove Turner
President

HT:dg

193

195

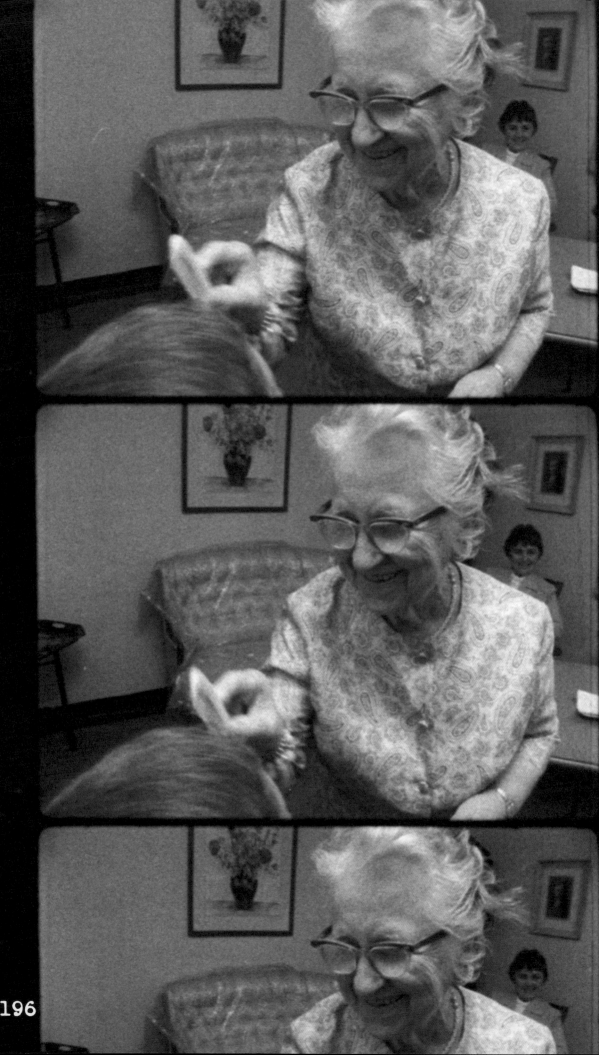

196

200

201

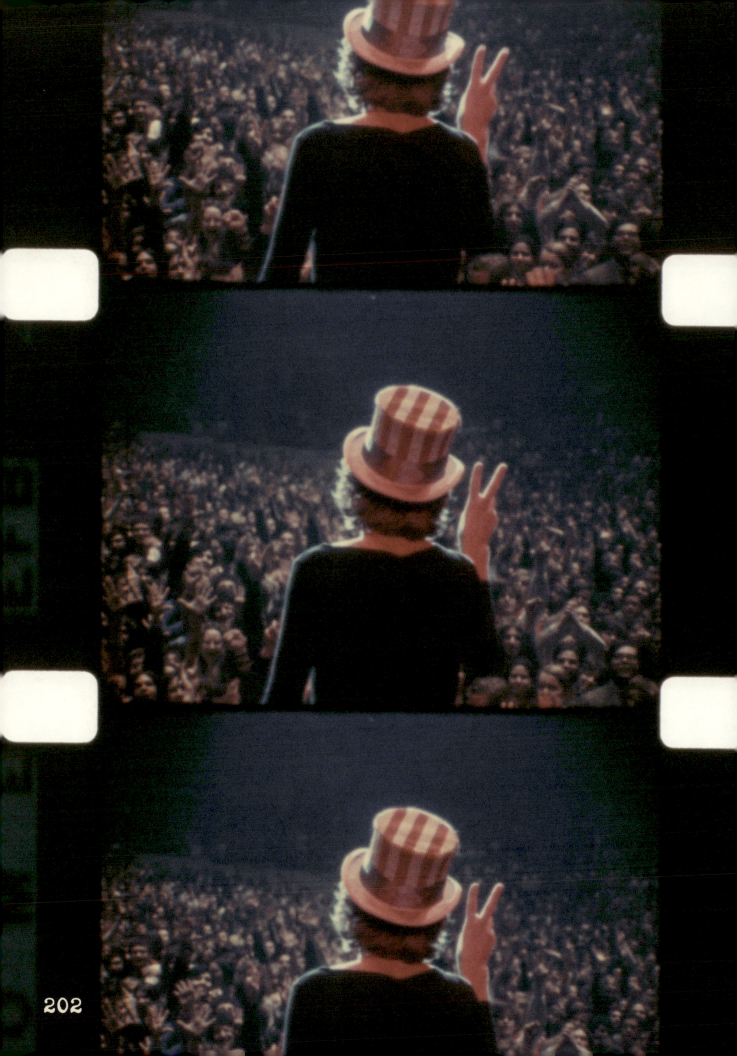

202

203

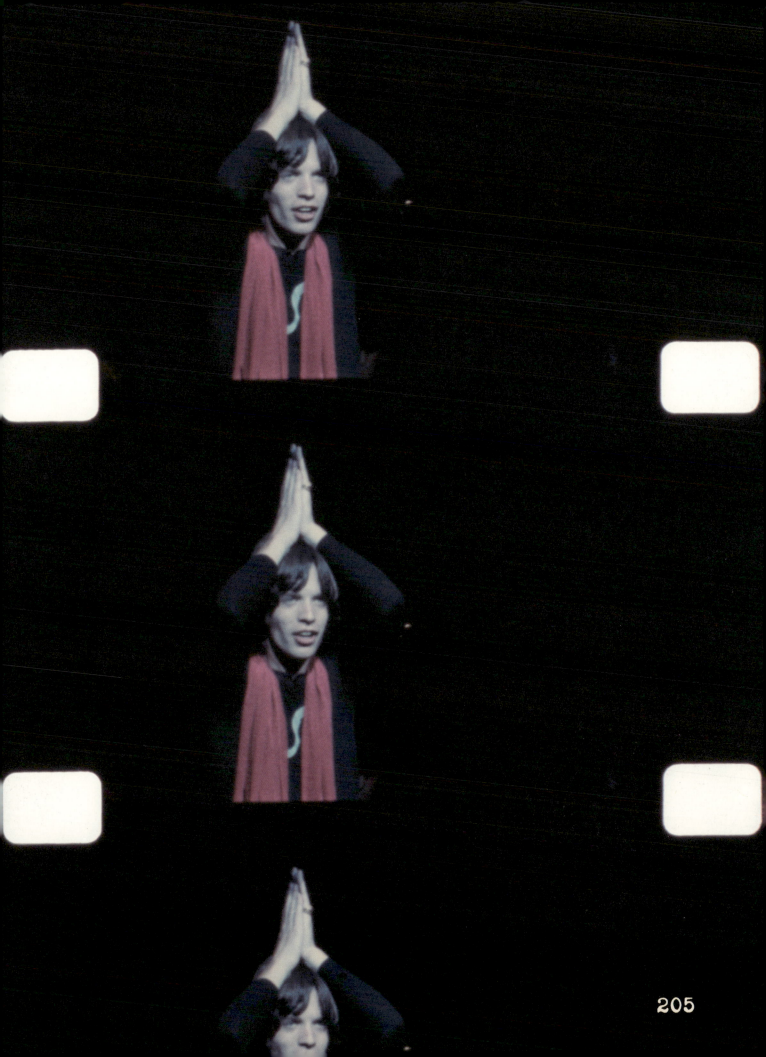

205

206

207

208

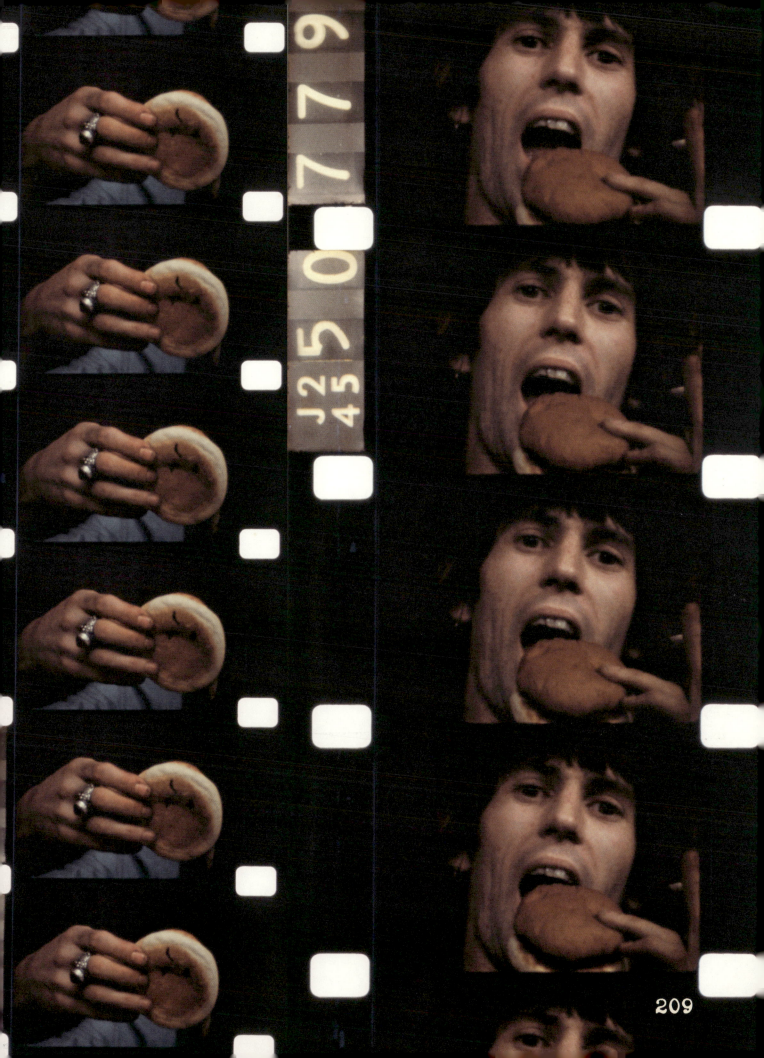

209

211

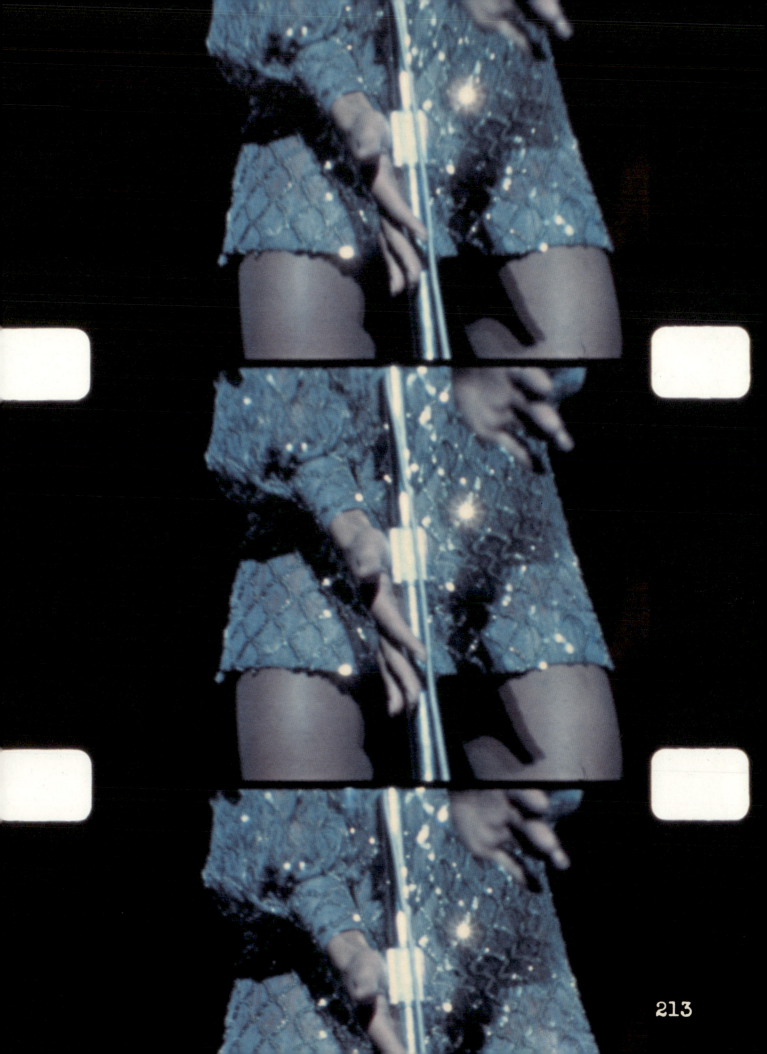

213

214

215

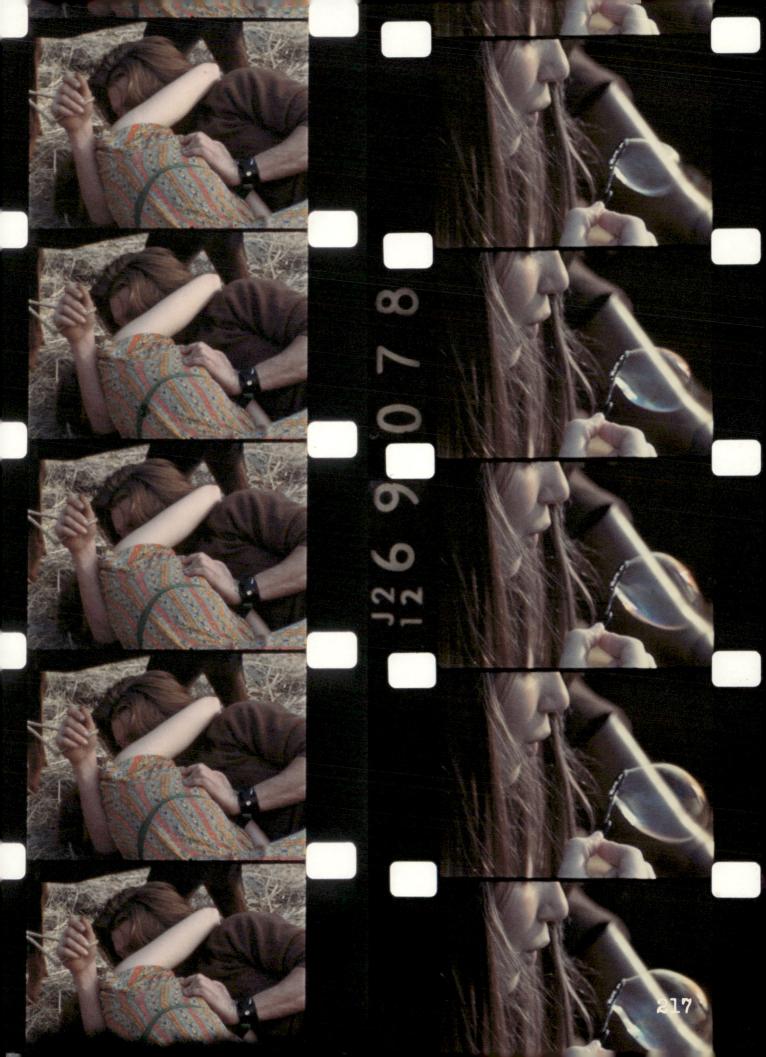

218

219

220

221

222

223

224

225

226

227

228

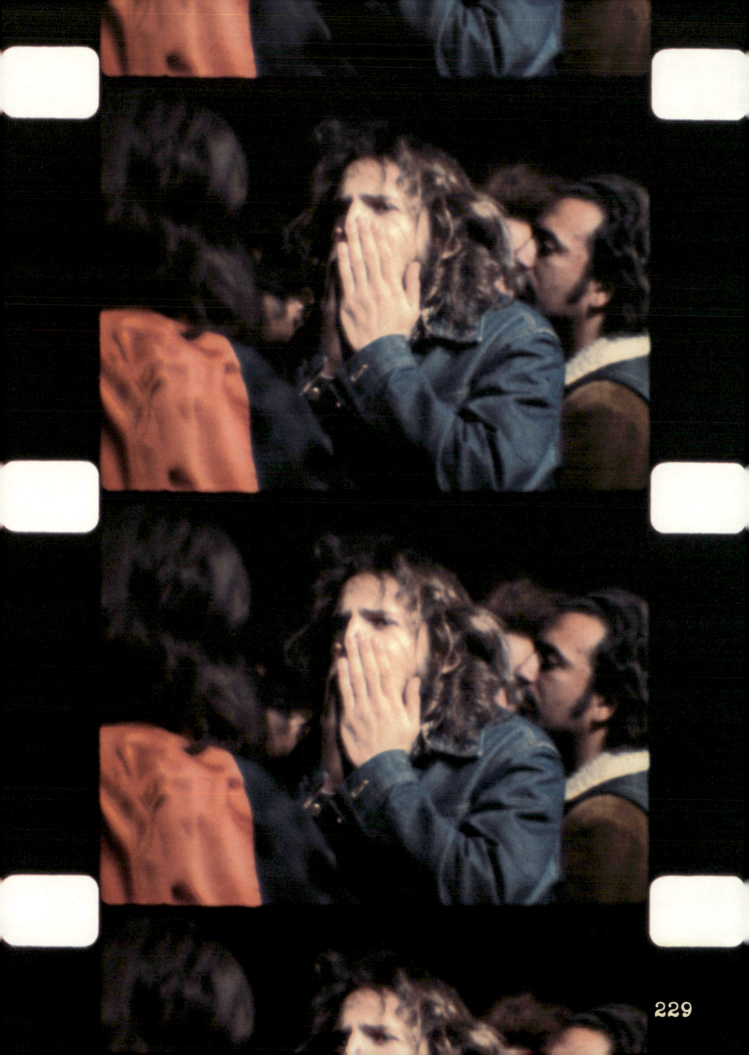

229

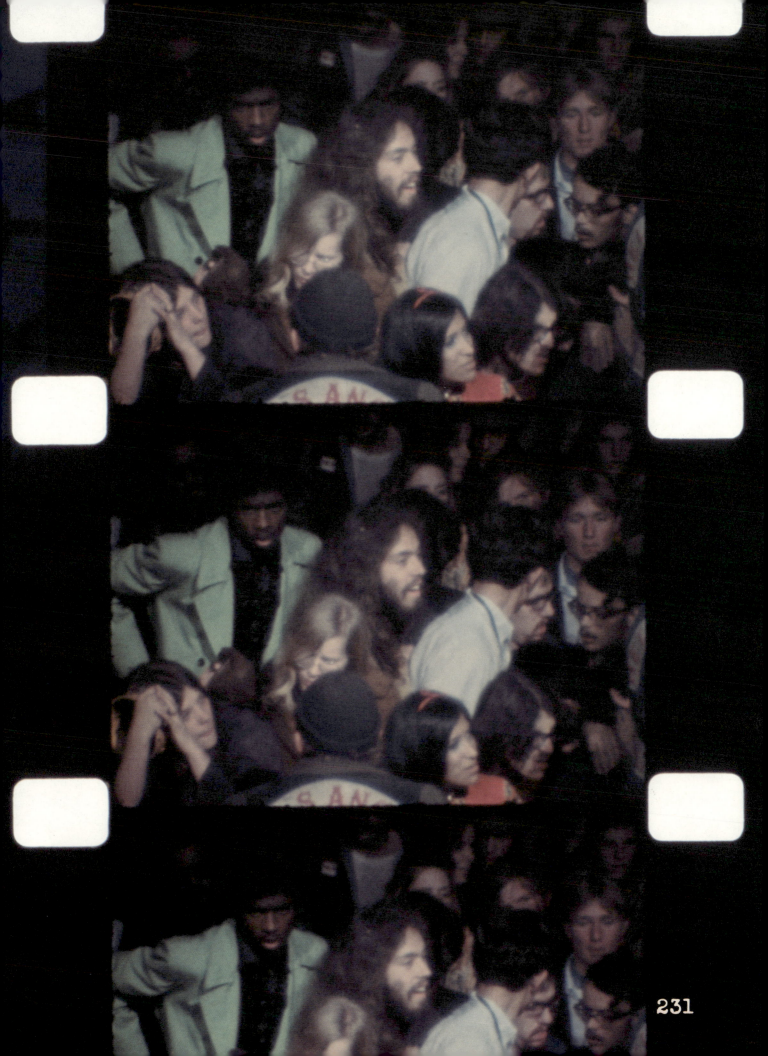

231

232

233

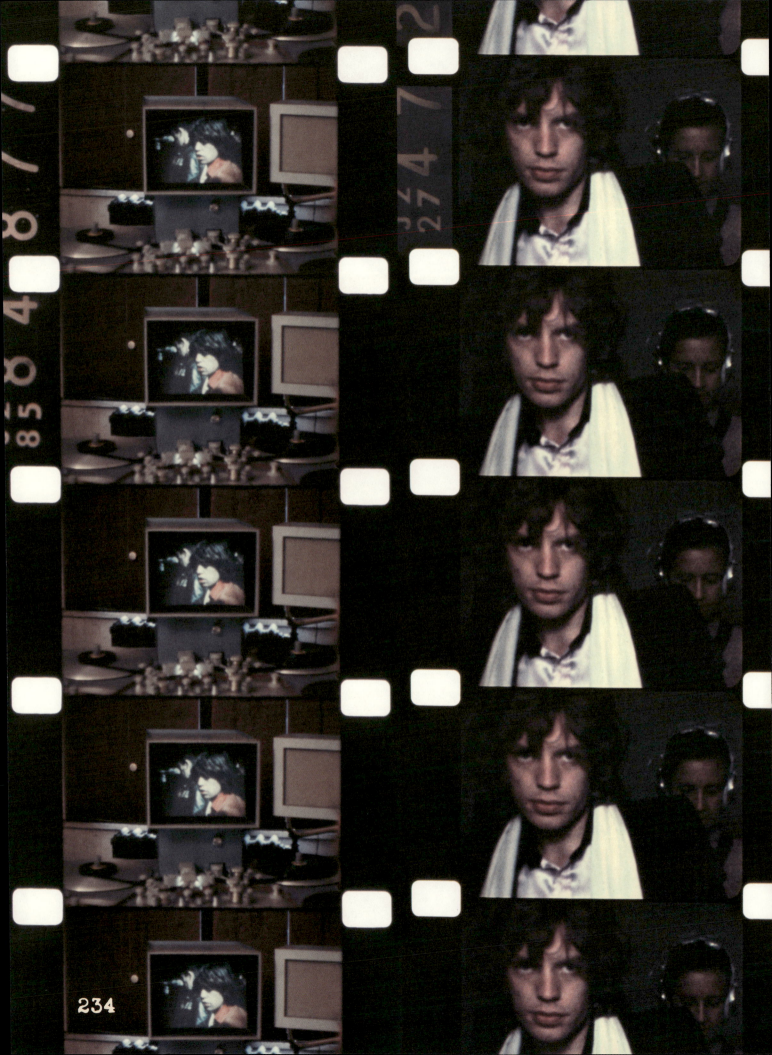

235

Tuesday, June 3rd.

Mick:

Here is a concrete plan (no more filming necessary)
for what I think will make for a better film that we all can
be proud of. It takes care of your main objection, i.e.
the picture is a horror, shocker leaving the audience
drained without - etc. Instead of being a philosopher
behind the movieola, now you can leave the audience
with whatever feeling you feel (via your own artistic
medium) in a song.

The new edit: After the incident actually occurs you
say "can we roll back for a minute" (as you say in
present version except in present version this comes
near the end). We roll back and do same slow motion
without your detailed comment - just the comment that
you couldn't see it from stage, didn't know about it
till after concert or whatever was the case. Then
the film continues to the last real-life scene - the
eerie scene of the people sort of falling down the
hillside. The last good frame of this scene is frozen.
(I've always wanted to end on this scene because it
just seemed right. At the freeze we begin to hear your
new song (or would a slow version of "Gimme Shelter"
be appropriate? Whatever song you feel you want to
leave the audience with). And continue with scenes
abstract, surreal or real. We have freedom here to
do it in one of several ways. The song itself can
give us the direction.

In addition, we cut out of the film the "Sam and Rock"
scene and the scene of you leaving edit machine at end.
We put in near the head of film Sam & Rock talking
about tradition of Angels at events in San Francisco.
Further, we tighten up the first half of the film
(editing which has been going on in N.Y. all the time
I've been here).

I would like to talk to you about the above just as soon
as possible. I'll be at the Inn On The Park (499 0888)

236

until I hear from you (if I step out will leave message
with Hall Porter).

Mick, I am very enthusiastic about the above as the
right direction to go. Hope you can see it....it's
a little difficult to put in print.

love.
David

Gimme Shelter: Production Notes

by ALBERT and DAVID MAYSLES

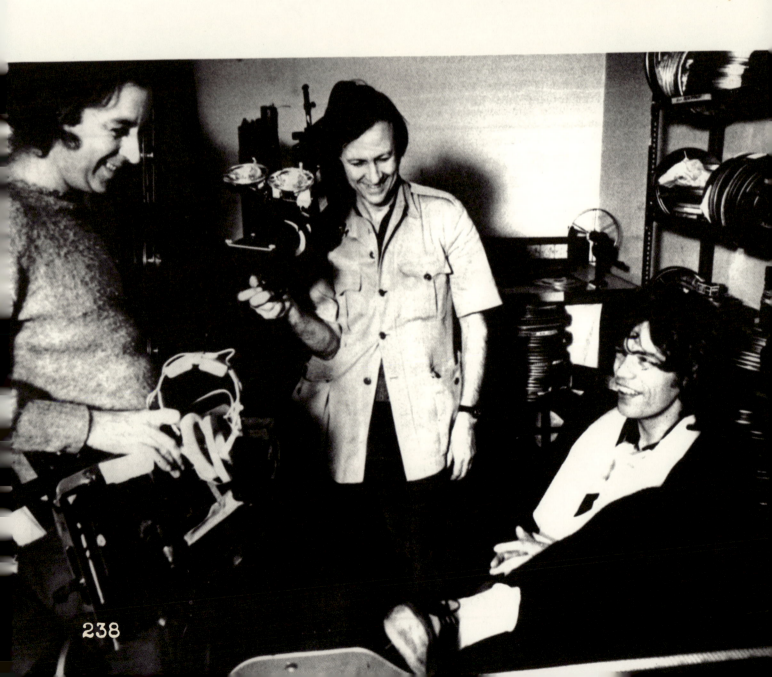

The Stones contacted us about shooting some footage of their Madison Square Garden concert which they would pay for. But we decided to stick with them on what little remained of their concert tour, filming when we saw fit and taking the financial risk ourselves with the hunch that we would make a film story of more than just rock concerts. It should be obvious to anyone who has seen SALESMAN that we wouldn't make just a concert film if there weren't other elements, beside the spectacle, which attracted us. Big spectacles do not generally interest us. Nor, for that matter, does violence. GIMME SHELTER has both, but when the violence, including the stabbing, occurred at Altamont, we were filming it as part of a developing story of the Stones' experience on and off stage in America, not for the shock or glamor, which are not enough to sustain a good feature.

When we arrived in California, we did not know we were going to shoot until the very last moment. We had to have additional cameramen on such short notice that we couldn't get more than one or two whose work we knew. One cameraman shot 6 or 7 rolls and nothing came out. Two others drank wine that was being passed out and couldn't work. The wine had LSD in it. All the camera teams were operating under very hazardous conditions—pushing, shoving, fighting, Hells Angels on and around the stage whose behavior was unpredictable.

We were all damn scared. Hence the title, "Gimme Shelter." The lyrics to that song are quite appropriate in expressing our feeling. It was the safe, pastoral world of friends, music, relaxation, and food invaded by the grotesque, the Hell's Angels. It turned out to be a classic subject, although we could not know that ahead of time. When the Stones came on stage, thousands of people were so crowded together we couldn't move at all, but we were in a good position in front of the stage and looking straight into their eyes, as we prefer to do. At this point, a man with two children sitting directly below Al was afraid the camera (on Al's shoulder) would fall on them, and he said that if Al didn't move out of his way in 20 seconds he was going to kill him. Fortunately somebody saw the predicament and pulled Al out of there and onto the stage. Later on it was exactly where he had stood that the stabbing took place. Sometimes we saw the Angels committing acts of violence and other times helping us with our equipment. We all seek answers: It was the Angels, or the Stones, money or the "superstar trip" which was responsible for the stabbing. But it was really much more complicated than that. We think the film shows just how complex it was.

The exposed footage for the film was about 100,000 feet—or a shooting ratio of about 38:1. Which is misleading. People may use the ratio to try to determine how objective the film is, or if it costs more to shoot this kind of film because so much has to be discarded. But no one ever asks a novelist how many pages of notes he discarded or chapters he deleted before the book was published.

We had many more poeple using cameras on this film than we normally do (usually it is just one camera), because there was music involved and the performance had to be covered from a number of angles. At Madison Square Garden we had five, and at Altamont about 10 cameras shooting film, most of which we could predict would not be used. But we wanted to be sure we had enough good footage on a number of songs. Years ago when we made a film with the Beatles (before "Hard Day's Night"), there was very little music performance and all the shooting was done just by us. We used one camera and the ratio came out to about 6:1.

We shot in 16 and blew it up to 35. The content of what you are filming dictates the method. In GIMME SHELTER, apart from the greater cost, 35mm equipment would have been too cumbersome. With 16, we can use lenses that have wider apertures than 35. We used the Angenieux 9.5-95, f2.2 zoom lens. To get that range in 35, the zoom lens would be much heavier and, worse than that, only f2.8 or 3.2 or 3.5, so you would be losing a stop or two. For the kind of things we do, we need a zoom and every bit of lens opening we can get. If we don't have it in the lens, then we have to start pushing the film, introducing grain and thereby degrading the film (and 35 pushed two stops is worse than 16 not pushed). The benefit of having the larger image area of 35 in the original would be lost by having to use lenses that would not give us enough light. The same, though a little less so, would apply to using Super-16.

Most important for our kind of shooting is a quiet camera—quieter than any 35. We use a camera Al built using an Auricon claw. It is very quiet, and nothing on the camera obscures the cameraman's 180 degree vision at any time. The cameraman is no longer an impersonal object stuck behind a machine; he is in everyone's view and can view everyone he is filming. This camera needs no brace because it balances perfectly on the shoulder, and it has no cable leading to or away from it.

LEFT: David Maysles, Albert Maysles, and Mick Jagger in London discussing rushes of GIMME SHELTER. (Photo by Stephen Goldblatt)

RIGHT: Stones drummer Charlie Watts and Charlotte Zwerin seated at the Steenbeck. (Photo by Albert Maysles)

239

We are working on a wire-free device which, when the camera is rolling the tape recorder will automatically be running while it also slates the film with a flash. The tape can still run without interruption before and after the camera starts and stops rolling. This will greatly reduce the amount of footage shot. A 40:1 ratio might become 25:1, because you can start and stop the camera at will and never have to keep the camera running when you don't want to (as you do when filming slates at the end of each take). We like to shoot only what we really want; to do otherwise is extremely demoralizing.

GIMME SHELTER was shot entirely handheld except for one camera position at the concerts in New York. We cannot even remember when we last used a tripod. Our shooting style has to do with the design of our camera as well as with our preoccupation with capturing things as they actually happen. When you use a tripod, you are immediately saying: "This is where *I* am. Now *you* move accordingly." It has to be the other way around. A fixed focus lens would do the same thing.

We shot in reversal color using a mixture of three stocks: 7255, 7242, and 7241. Now, however, we have replaced 7255 with 7252, which wasn't available at that time. The quality of it is vastly superior to 42 or 41. But all three have better quality than color negative, which a lot of poeple use because of its greater latitude. However, this stock is nowhere near as sharp as the reversal, and it is also very grainy.

At Altamount we had about 80 rolls of 7255 raw stock that never got to us. It was probably stolen. So, some of the time we had to shoot in bright daylight with 7242 or 41 because it was all we had. Normally the results would have been unsatisfactory because the contrast level (compared to 7255) would be very high when you blew up to 35. Instead, we had Consolidated Film Industries in Hollywood post-flash the original 7242 and 7241 to equate their contrast with the 7255. Some poeple think that this affects speed, but it doesn't. It might cost a little more, but it is certainly worth doing. We recommend this process especially if you are considering blowing up later on, since blowing up increases the contrast quite a bit, thus maximizing the importance of starting with a low-contrast stock.

When you expose and process color properly, you can get every bit as good, or better, results than with black and white. We used to be ardent lovers of black and white, but we do not feel that way now. Some people try to justify using black and white to get the higher speed you need when working in available light, but we have found that color film speeds are actually faster than black and white, especially in the combination of 52, 42, and 41. If you push 41 two stops, you get an ASA reading of 620—with quality better than any black and white pushed to that speed.

The Stones' concerts were lit by Chipmonck, who provided us with enough light to photograph. We never told him how to light it, nor did we know in advance what the lighting would be. Color balance was estimated at the time of shooting, since there was no anticipating what the color would be. Normally we carry a very large set of gelatins with us. People make a lot of mistakes with color filters. They put the gelatin behind the lens. This is wrong because it in effect displaces the lens from its proper position. This is true even though camera manufacturers build their cameras to have filters slots behind the lens in order to make filming easier. Arriflex puts glass in front of the lens, but this is wrong, too. We feel the best way is to use a gelatin filter, the thinner the better, very flat in front of the lens.

The music performances were recorded on a 16 track console. The final film is in 4-track stereo. There was enough space to lay down the 4 tracks by putting two on either side of the film, as it is conventionally done. Then Mr. Rugoff spent over $10,000 on the Plaza Theater putting in an enormous new screen and getting the sound right. When the film is shown outside New York City, however, the results have often been disastrous. There are problems with the projection, proper amplification, and placing of speakers. Once when the film opened out of town, we saw a projectionist 200 feet from the screen trying to focus it. When we asked him what he focused on, he said, "the picture." It would be better to focus on the grain of the film. But most projectionists totally reject this idea and will tell you, "I've been projecting films over 20 years and you're telling me ..." In Paris, when the film opened on the Champs Elysees, they ran the optical track on the 4-track magnetic print. (Because of the optical track's width and position on the 4-track mag print, there is a great loss in quality. It is on the film for emergency purposes only.) At times we have sent our own engineer, at our expense, to supervise the projection and sound balance—only to find that a day later it was all back to the usual way.

GIMME SHELTER cost more than a half million dollars to make. A big portion of this went for expenses you would not necessarily encounter on a feature on this type—that is, huge legal fees, long negotiations here, in California, and abroad for the purchase of music licenses, etc.

It might also be possible to make a very good feature with a budget of $50,000. Henri Lartigue, a still photographer, took some photographs that have become classics when he was only ten years old in 1910. He was a one-man crew, and he only knew that he wanted to take photographs. (Which is better than most filmmakers, who "know" too well—from studying too many movies?—how they are "supposed" to film). He was too young to have any preconceived ideas; all he had was the compulsion to tell his story, which was mostly of his family, in photographs. He expressed his art through the simplest of means, almost unconsciously, out of his personal interest. Although we are a two-man crew, this element, more than a large budget, is what we like to see in a film.

One of the reasons we have always financed our own feature films, aside from the fact that we believe it's the only way to have complete artistic control, is that it is very hard to get enthusiastic enough to convince a financier if you cannot guarantee him what the final film will look like. (The very nature of our films would preclude our being interested in a film where we could "guarantee" the result.) We have never had to abandon a film before completion, but it could happen. However, if this same film was financed by someone other than ourselves, that person would more than likely insist on a finished film so that he could at least recoup his investment. We never want to be in a position where we are forced to complete something. Just recently we were discussing another film with the Stones, and they agreed completely with this. And if we do start one, we will only raise outside money at the point when we *know* we are going to complete the film. We had a good relationship with the Stones because we respect each other as perfectionists. There is no limit to the time or money we will spend to get the results we want. And we are fortunate to have Charlotte Zwerin, who feels the same way, working with us. Our stereo mix took 18 days and, including the preparation, the sound track cost more than $75,000.

Why do we make films anyway? Because we get a great deal of satisfaction out of telling the story just the way we see it, not as preconceived but from what we experienced watching it unfold. Was the stabbing in the film "exploiting a murder," as some have suggested? We never judged it as a "murder." Those who did could not wait for the jury trial which concluded a verdict of "self defense," not premeditated homicide. This goes to the heart of what we are trying to do in our films: letting what happens happen without interfering in any way. A faith (some call it a fanatic dicipline. Maybe it is.) in life as is, is more interesting material for films and more valid than anything we could possibly invent.

"MAKING MURDER PAY?" is the title of Vincent Canby's cynical front page article in this section on December 13th about our film, "Gimme Shelter" now at the Plaza theater. He calls us humanists but says he is depressed by "the exuberant opportunism with which it (the movie) exploits the events" in refering to Altamont and the killing. "It probably would have been a kind of mini-Woodstock," he says, describing what the film would have been without the killing, which he later calls a "murder".

Altamont and the killing in front of the stage happened. It was not Woodstock!

The fictionalization of violence has certainly been accepted as a legitimate subject. In our film a real killing has been photographed and is shown along with other events at Altamont in the order in which they happened. This non-fiction Mr. Canby finds exploitive and opportunistic.

In the interest of reporting what actually happened, the film shows the victim with a gun in his hand before he was stabbed. TIMES readers should know that the trial of the man wielding the knife in the film had not begun when the bold print "MAKING MURDER PAY?" appeared over Mr. Canby's piece. (The trial is in progress now and a murder conviction has not been reached as of this writing.) We hope these same readers will see our film and not take his other charges as the truth but draw their own conclusions.

The space we have been given, although appreciated, precludes our

answering all his charges in detail. In "Salesman", we did not put the Bible salesmen "into artificial situations" nor "send them to Miami" anymore than we wrote the Stones' songs and sent them to Altamont. The Stones say they did not hire the Angels. The Angels say they were not hired.

Mr. Canby writes, "I can't help but feel that someone thought, 'Wow! What luck!' when it was found that Meredith Hunter's death had been filmed."

What incredible cynicism!

Our feelings about Altamont are in the film.

David Maysles, Albert Maysles, Charlotte Zwerin

245

247

249

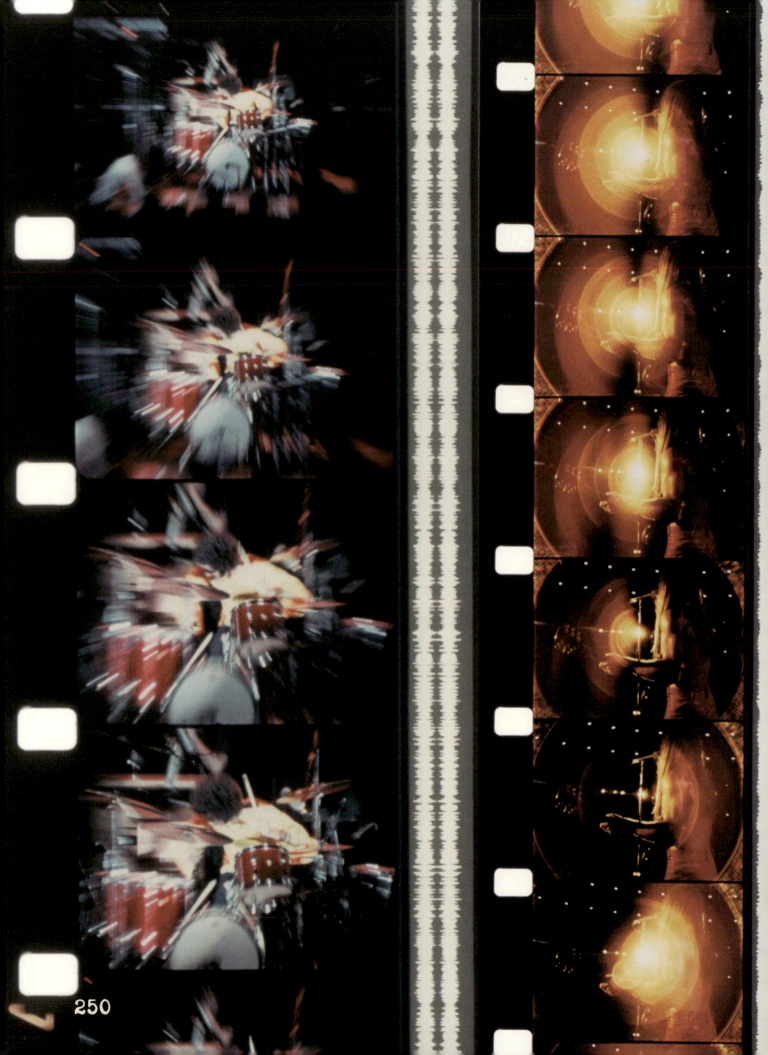

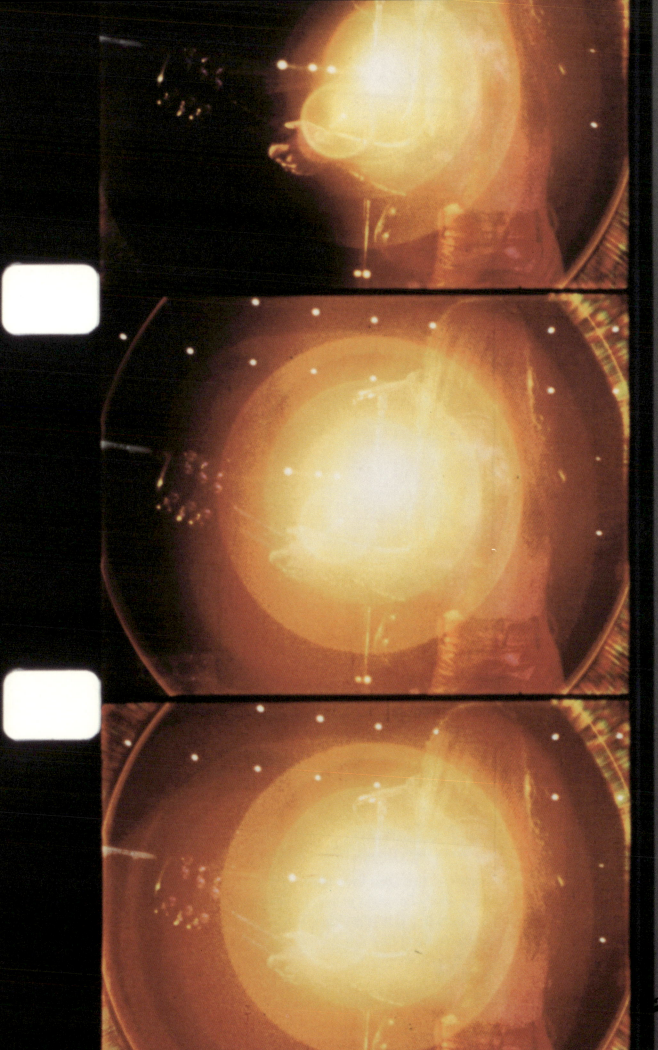

251

valley curtain 1973

Christo's Valley Curtain

Christo's Valley Curtain

Christo's Valley Curtain

"Valley Curtain," Rifle, Colorado, 1970-72, © Christo 1972.

Photo: Wolfgang Volz

Iron-workers risk their lives hanging a quarter-mile of orange curtain across a windy Colorado valley. In the process, they discover Art. As one worker puts it: "This is a vision, boy—I would never in a lifetime think of doing anything like this."

A film by
Albert Maysles, David Maysles and Ellen Hovde

MAYSLES FILMS, INC.

252

CHRISTO'S VALLEY CURTAIN

A FILM BY THE MAYSLES BROTHERS AND ELLEN HOVDE

NOMINATED FOR AN ACADEMY AWARD

"Christo's Valley Curtain," (by Albert and David Maysles and Ellen Hovde) is marvelous reportage of the sort the Maysles brothers do best...The surprise of the film is the enthusiasm with which this project was greeted by the residents of the town of Rifle (pop. 2,150) and by the construction workers who risked limbs and lives on the stunt. Says one hardhat: "It's not the erection of it [that's important], it's the thought."

—Vincent Canby, *NEW YORK TIMES*

David and Albert Maysles' "Valley Curtain" is by far the finest film I have ever seen about an artist and his work. Technically brilliant, beautifully paced, with not an image wasted or held too long, the film somehow makes it possible for the viewer to become involved at a deep and personal level with the whole mad, marvelous epic. "Valley Curtain" is never didactic; it neither explains nor describes, and this is its great strength. On its own terms the film is as novel, as surprising, as hilarious, and in the end as beautiful as the work of art with which it deals.

Calvin Tomkins
NEW YORKER magazine

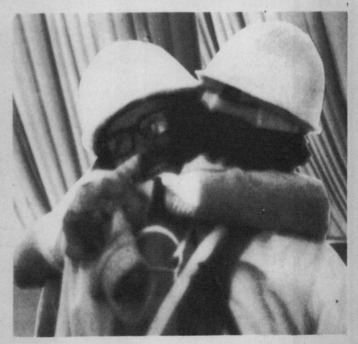

"IN THE 25 YEARS I'VE BEEN VIEWING ART FILMS, I BELIEVE THAT THIS MUST BE THE BEST."

—Ned Griner, Head, Art Department
BALL STATE UNIVERSITY

The Burk Family Of Georgia

Maysles Films, Inc.
1697 Broadway at 53rd
New York, N.Y. 10019

A Film By

David Maysles **Albert Maysles** **Ellen Hovde** **Muffie Meyer**

Produced by/Maysles Films, Inc.

Monday, May 9

Six American Families

Executive Producer/George Moynahan
Westinghouse Broadcasting Co.

8:30 P.M., Channel 13

Photograph: Marianne Barcellona

May 24, 1977

Dr. Calvin Kimbrough
Director
Candler School of Theology Media Center
Atlanta, Georgia

Dear Dr. Kimbrough

I read of your objection to the use of subtitles in the film of the Burk family of Dalton, Georgia. We fought against them, too, and for the same reasons. But since it was a commissioned film that choice was not ours. Television still operates out of a sense of fear that somehow neither subject nor audience has the ability to go it alone. In our other films, non-commissioned, SALESMAN and GREY GARDENS, for example, subjects and audience do go it alone: one reason TV won't show them.

Thank you for insisting on what we also believe and execute when we can. Unfortunately, because someone else paid for it this film was only 90%, not 100% our own.

Sincerely,

Albert Maysles

M/nls

THE
GREAT SINGER
"BIG" EDITH
BOUVIER
BEALE

THE
GREAT DANCER
EDITH "LITTLE EDIE"
BOUVIER
BEALE II

Signs: Lois Wright

"Part of the fascination, of course, has to do with the resemblances one sees between the Beales and their niece/first cousin Jacqueline Bouvier Kennedy Onassis."
Vincent Canby, *New York Times*

"It's a hell of a show. Incredible. Hilarious, horrifying and tragic all at once."
Bernard Drew, *Gannett Newspapers*

"An astonishing study of two women who have retreated from the world into a time warp of their own."
Jack Kroll, *Newsweek*

"GREY GARDENS" offers a powerful display of reality far more involving and poetic than most fiction. Reality and fantasy become inseparable. It is as compelling a drama as Tennessee Williams might achieve."
William Wolf, *Cue Magazine*

"Remarkable," Howard Kissel, *Women's Wear Daily*
"Extraordinary," John Crittenden, *The Record*
"Fantastique," *Paris Match*
"People are talking about 'Grey Gardens'.... It is devastating."
Charlotte Curtis, *Vogue Magazine*

Design: John Anthes and J. Michael McNeil

"They had this incredible, spontaneous repartee going between them all the time," says Al, explaining why the Maysles were attracted to the Beales. "One of them would talk and the other would contradict her or compete with her for the listener's attention. And what they were talking about was rooted in such basic things--about a failure to break away from home, about an inability to break with the past. At the same time, both women were connected to nature and beauty and art."

It was, in part, because they were both unfulfilled performers that the Beales made such wonderful subjects. Mrs. Beale fancied herself a professional singer. Edie had modeled with an eye on the theater. "They were not accomplished artists," says David, "but they had the temperament and outlook of artists and the performer's instinct; they seemed to know intuitively that sing-ing 'Tea for Two' was the perfect thing to do." On the other hand, the Maysles had to put up with a coyness that would have discouraged less persistent filmmakers. "They would play a cat and mouse game with us," says Al. "We'd arrive for shooting and be told by Edie that her mother couldn't be filmed because she hadn't bathed. (Once Mrs. Beale joked, "I haven't taken a bath in ten years.") But a few minutes later, Edie would invite us in.

262

The five filmmakers who made GREY GARDENS

GG #1

Left to right, back row: David Maysles, Ellen Hovde, Albert Maysles
Front row: Muffie Meyer, Susan Froemke

270

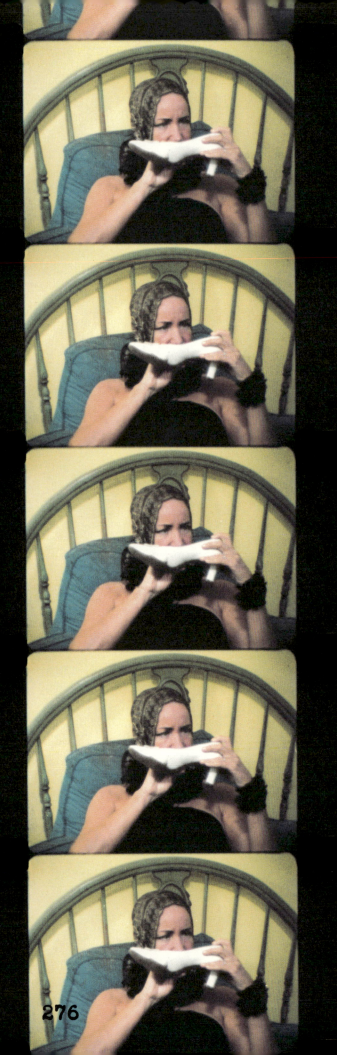

276

278

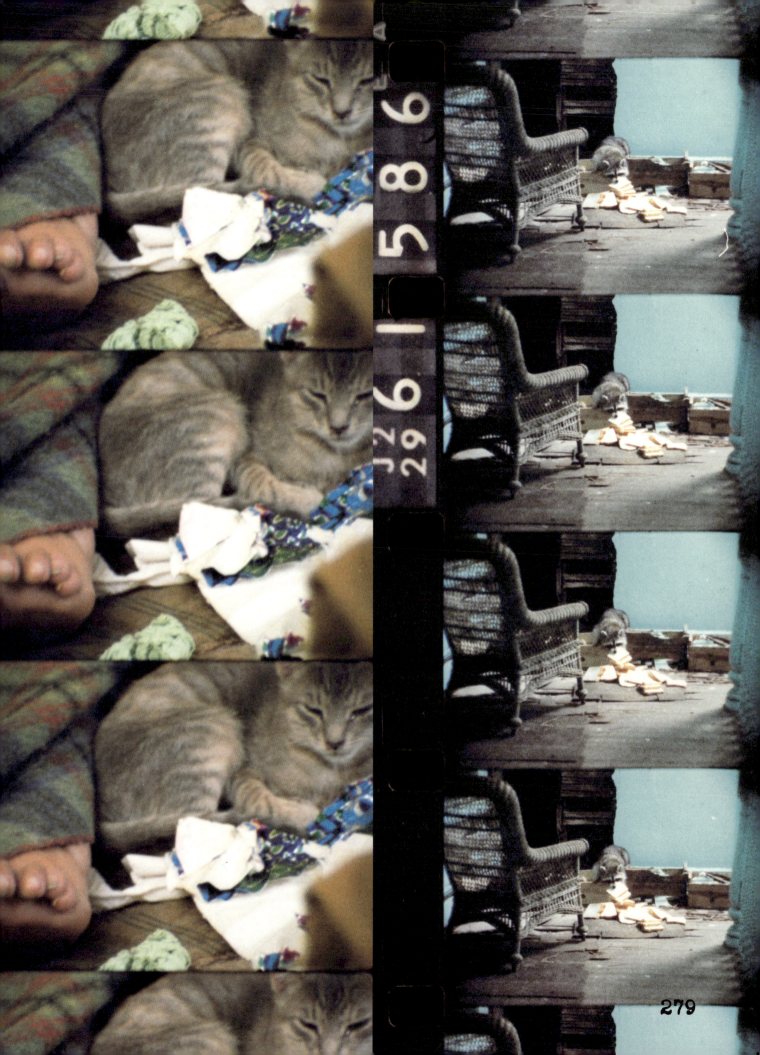

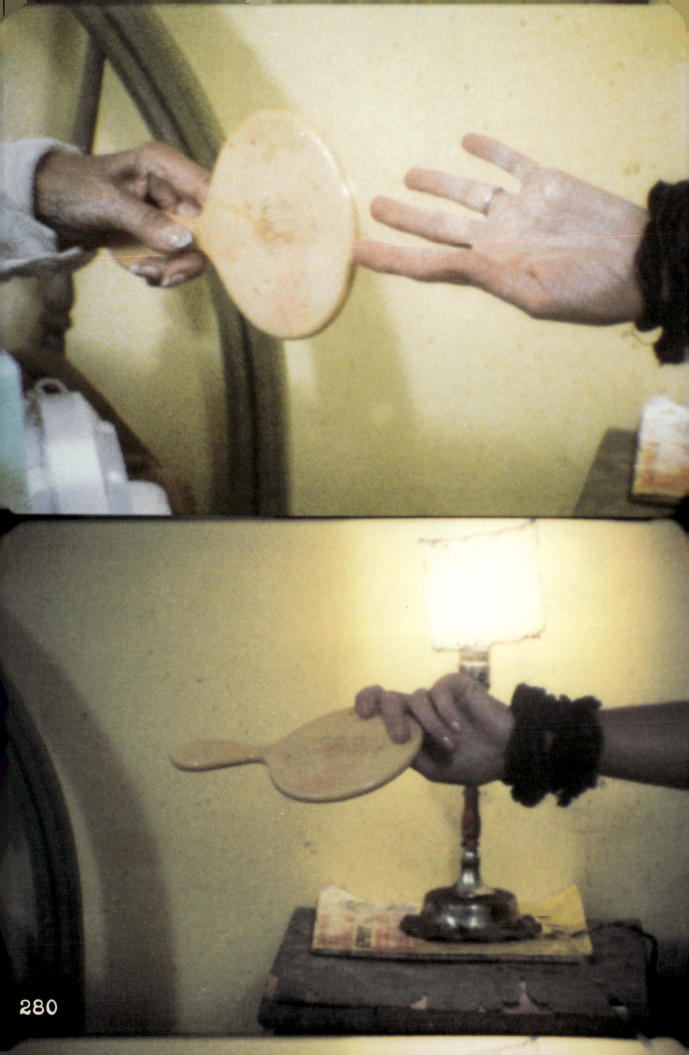

281

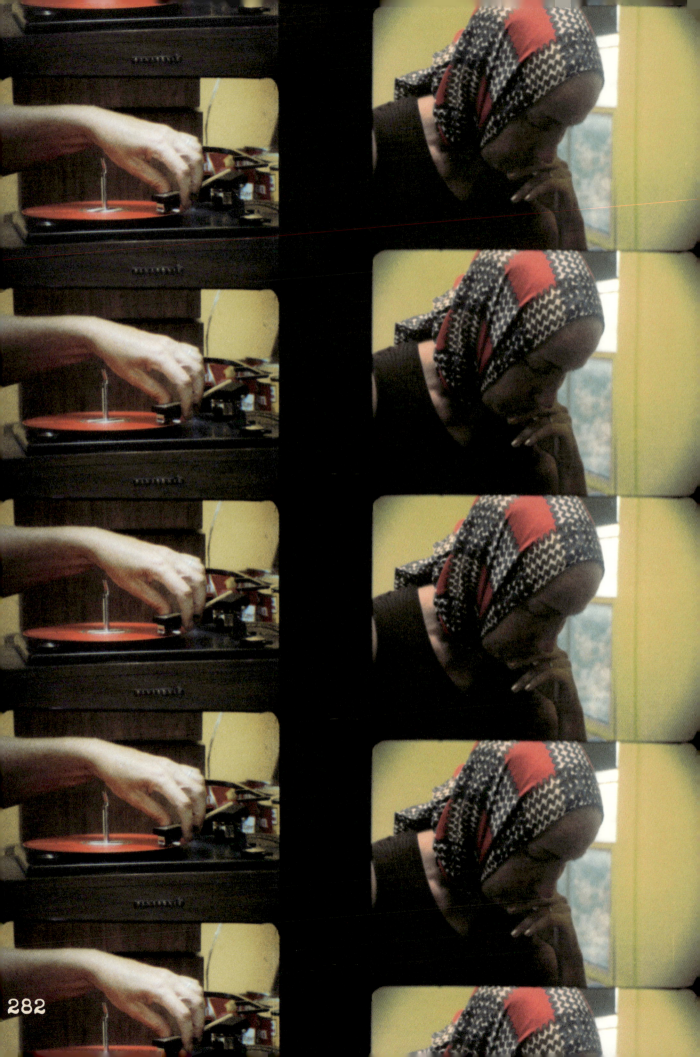

286

Edie: (to Maysles) It's very difficult to keep the line
               between the past and the present. You know what I
               mean? It's awfully difficult.

                              * * *

Edie: I suppose I won't get out of here until she dies or
               I die.

Mrs. Beale: Who's "she"--the cat? Why do you want to get out?
               Any place would be much worse.

Edie: Yeah. But I like freedom.

Mrs. Beale: Well you can't get any freedom when you're being
               supported.

Edie: I think you're not free when you're not being
               supported. It's awful both ways.

Mrs. Beale: When are you gonna learn, Edie, you're in this world;
               you're not out of the world . . .

Edie: Mother, you don't have enough clothes on.

Mrs. Beale: Well, I'm gonna get naked in just a minute so you'd
               better watch out.

Edie: That's what I'm afraid of.

Mrs. Beale: Yeah. Now why? I haven't got any warts on me.

Photo of Albert
& David Maysles

Edie: One of my cats
                     just got out.

David Maysles: Edie, you look
                     fantastic.

BACK YARD in
field of
clematis

Edie: David, you look absolutely terrific, Honestly.
                 You've got light, you've got light blue on. Well,
                 Al, you're still, ah . . . Mother says you're very
                 conservative (laughs). Brooks, everything looks
                 wonderful.

Brooks: Thank you.

Edie: Absolutely wonderful. This is the best thing
                 to wear for today. You understand.

David Maysles: Yeah.

Edie: Because I don't like women in skirts, and the
                 best thing is to wear pantyhose or some pants
                 under a short skirt, I think. Then you have the
                 pants under the skirt, and then you can pull the
                 stockings up over the pants, underneath the skirt.

Albert Maysles: Uh-huh . . .

Edie: And you can always take off the skirt and use it
                 as a cape. So I think this is the best costume
                 for the day.

Albert Maysles: OK.

288

Edie: (laughs) I have to think these things up, you know. Mother wanted me to come out in a kimona so we had quite a fight. So what did you do, photograph Brooks cutting right down here?

Albert Maysles: Yeah. I've Been through the jungle.

Edie: Oh, for goodness sakes. What do you want to do now . . . . where do you want to go? Upstairs? You want to go up and photograph it from the top porch?

David Maysles: OK.

Edie: OK. They're gonna photograph from the top now, Brooks.

WALK thru
bushes into
Back Porch
area

David Maysles: It's a beautiful garden back here.

Edie: Did you see the wall garden? Oh, you mean the patio--you mean this.

David Maysles: Yeah.

Edie: That's a Spanish wall garden over there, you know.

David Maysles: Oh, yes.

Edie: The Hills put that in. They imported everything from Rome. Mrs. Hill, she was a famous horti-culturist. That was one of the famous gardens of America. Brooks, next summer if we're all living, I think a vegetable garden would be a good thing in here.

291

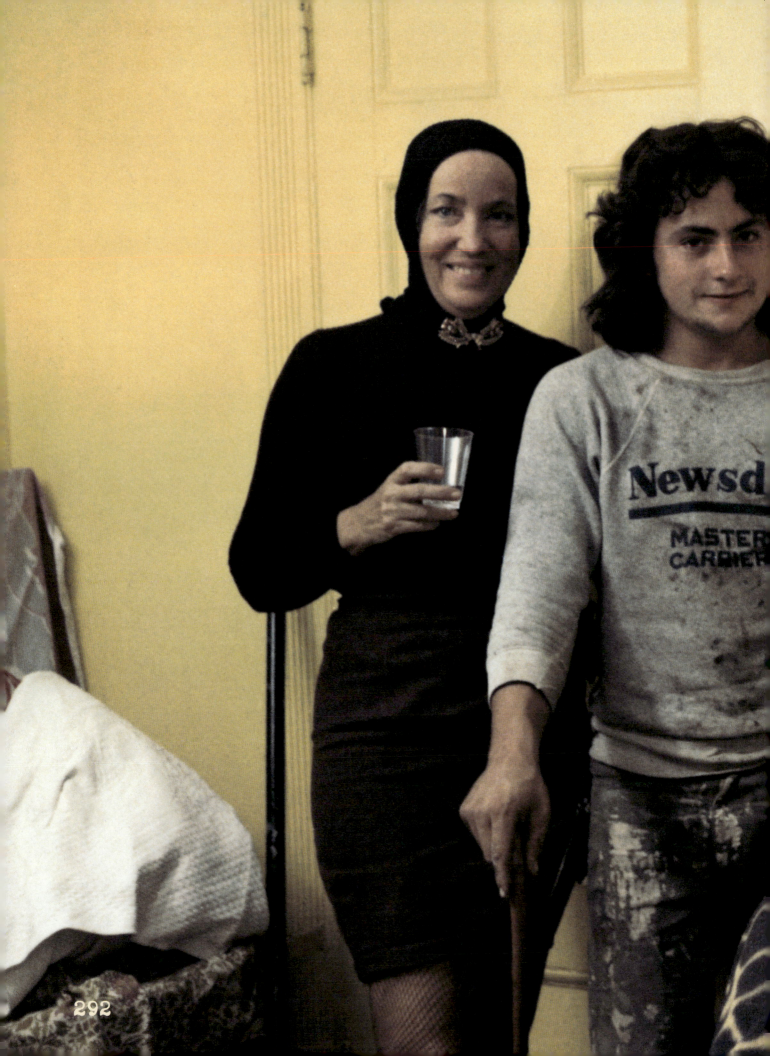

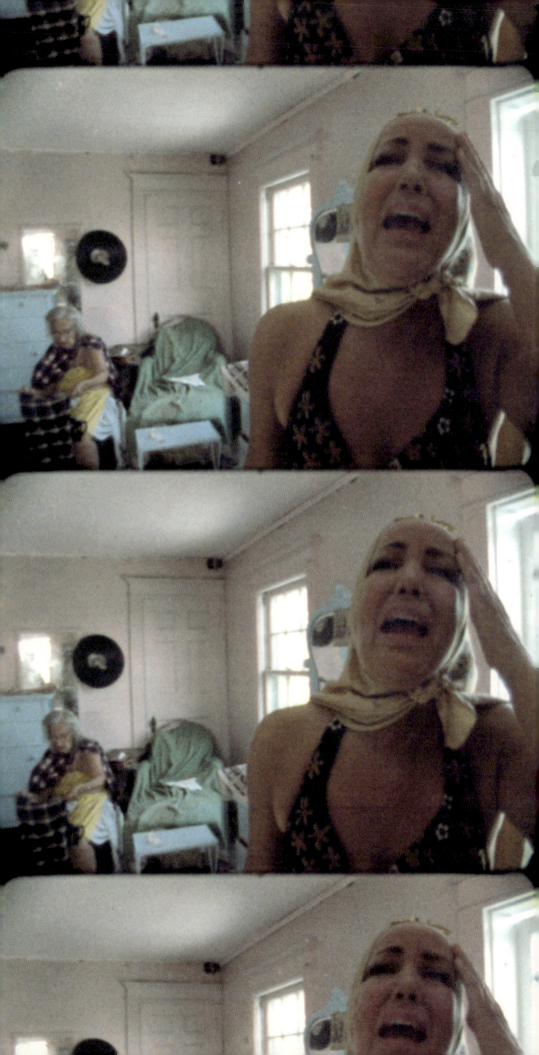

297

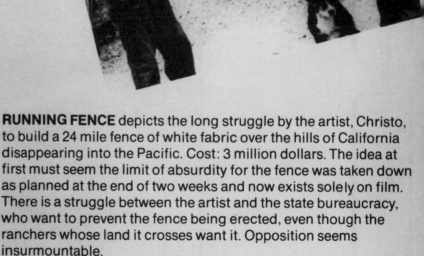

A MAYSLES' FILM PRODUCTION

Running Fence

By **DAVID MAYSLES** **CHARLOTTE ZWERIN** **ALBERT MAYSLES**

American Film Institute
The John F. Kennedy Center
for the Performing Arts
Washington, D. C. 20566

Dear Albert, David, and Charlotte:

Your presentation last week was one of the outstanding events of our Tenth Anniversary Celebration. I was so glad you agreed to give us a
first look at RUNNING FENCE, which I found an
enthralling experience. No film I have seen
captures so well the struggle to create a work
of art nor interprets that work with such an
imagination.

With many thanks,

Sincerely,

Michael Webb,
Director
National Film Gallery

300

RUNNING FENCE depicts the long struggle by the artist, Christo, to build a 24 mile fence of white fabric over the hills of California disappearing into the Pacific. Cost: 3 million dollars. The idea at first must seem the limit of absurdity for the fence was taken down as planned at the end of two weeks and now exists solely on film. There is a struggle between the artist and the state bureaucracy, who want to prevent the fence being erected, even though the ranchers whose land it crosses want it. Opposition seems insurmountable.

The fence finally unfurled brings the community together in celebration of its beauty. After four years of work, Christo sees his vision realized. "See how it describes the wind."

"The beauty of the curtains blowing in the wind as the fence comes out of the sea and runs across the hills and meadows of California is to me one of the most moving sights I have seen. There are town meetings which I think show America at its very best. And then there is the enthusiasm of the young people building the fence. I must say I was moved quite literally to tears. I came to the conclusion the fence is a work of art, and I believe the film is also."

John Walker
Director Emeritus
National Gallery of Art
Washington, D.C.

"RUNNING FENCE picks up where GIMME SHELTER left off. GIMME SHELTER, the Maysles Brothers (with Charlotte Zwerin) Altamont film, dealt with the breakdown of community, the exhaustion of the youth culture of the '60s; RUNNING FENCE, their new movie, in a sense deals with the survival of community, the way in which people discover the meaning of integrity and integration through a creative act."

— Robert Taylor, *THE BOSTON GLOBE*

301

Running Fence

It's beautiful. Look.
Look.   Look at that.

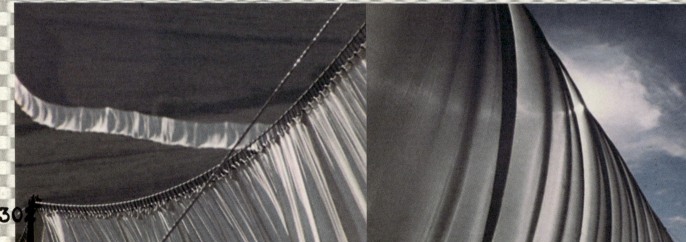

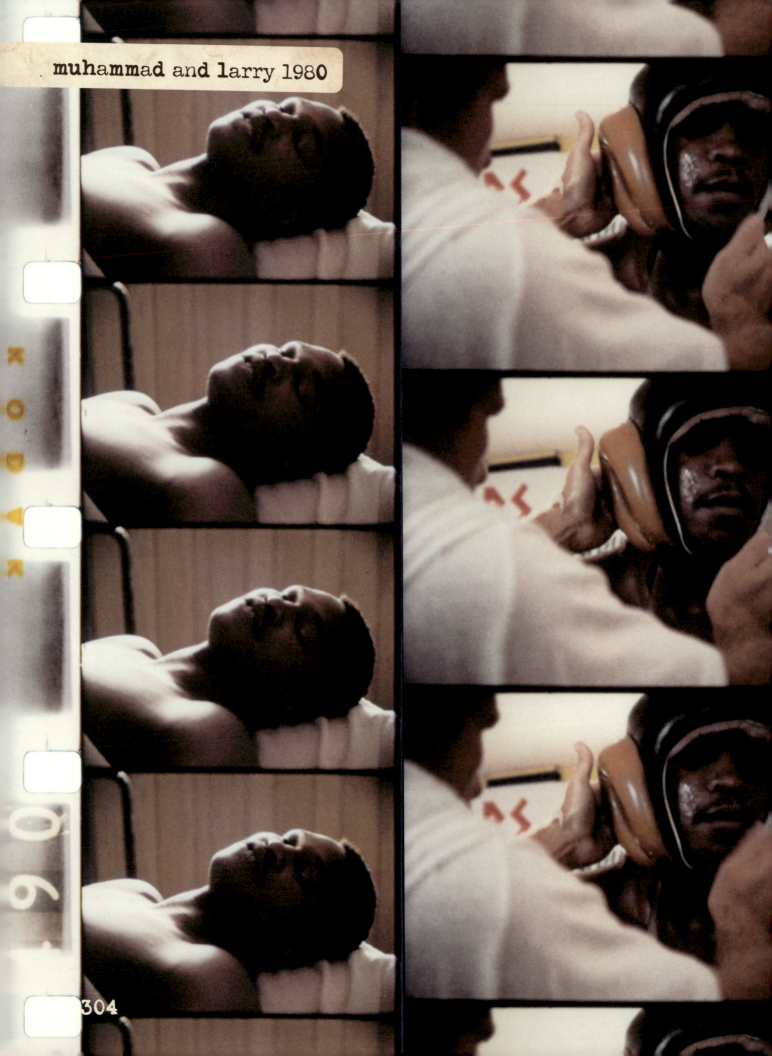

muhammad and larry 1980

305

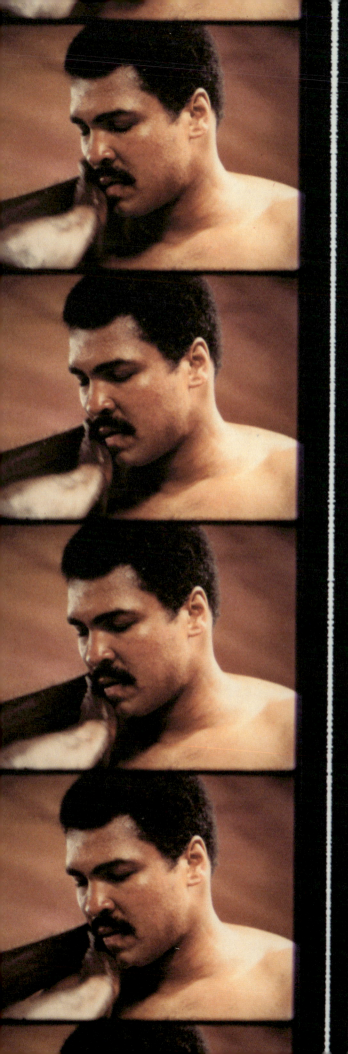
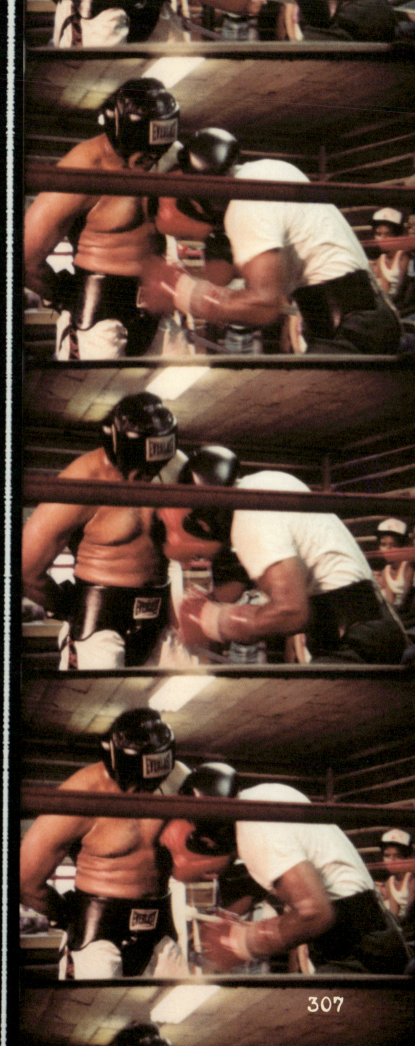

ozawa 1985

This highly acclaimed 1985 documentary by leading American filmmakers Albert and David Maysles has as its subject conductor Seiji Ozawa and captures the behind-the-scenes drama of the world of the symphony orchestra.

Focusing on the fascinating life of Ozawa as we follow his conducting schedule encompassing three continents, this one-hour documentary suggests the lifestyle of any of the leading conductors of the last 20th century.

The film communicates the intensity and passion that Ozawa brings to his work. It is also a portrait of Ozawa as both student and teacher, exploring these roles in his relationships with former masters and in his current struggles with his own Tanglewood students.

Shot on location at Tanglewood, Salzburg, Berlin, Tokyo, and Osaka, the film presents an intimate portrait of Ozawa as a musician through his work as music director of the Boston Symphony and his musical projects in Japan, as well as in his private life with his wife and children.

The film begins at Tanglewood with Ozawa preparing Mahler's Symphony No. 2, which he and the Boston Symphony will bring to Salzburg and Berlin later that summer. Featured are Jessye Norman and Edith Weins in rehearsal and performance. Also featured in the film are cellist Yo-Yo Ma in Salzburg, Rudolph Serkin in Tanglewood, and Herbert von Karajan, whom Ozawa meets early one morning in Salzburg as von Karajan prepares to pilot his jet from Salzburg to St. Tropez.

The film also examines the incidents that resulted in Ozawa's rejection of Japan as he was beginning his career and his subsequent decision to leave, launching his career in the West.

The Maysles are known for working within the *cinema verite* style, which has come to represent filmmaking that captures reality as it happens. It is a unique

presentation of classical music for a television audience as musical segments are interwoven within the context of Ozawa's life.

308

OZAWA is a production of CAMI VIDEO in association with Antenne 2, NHK, ZDF and CBS Sony.

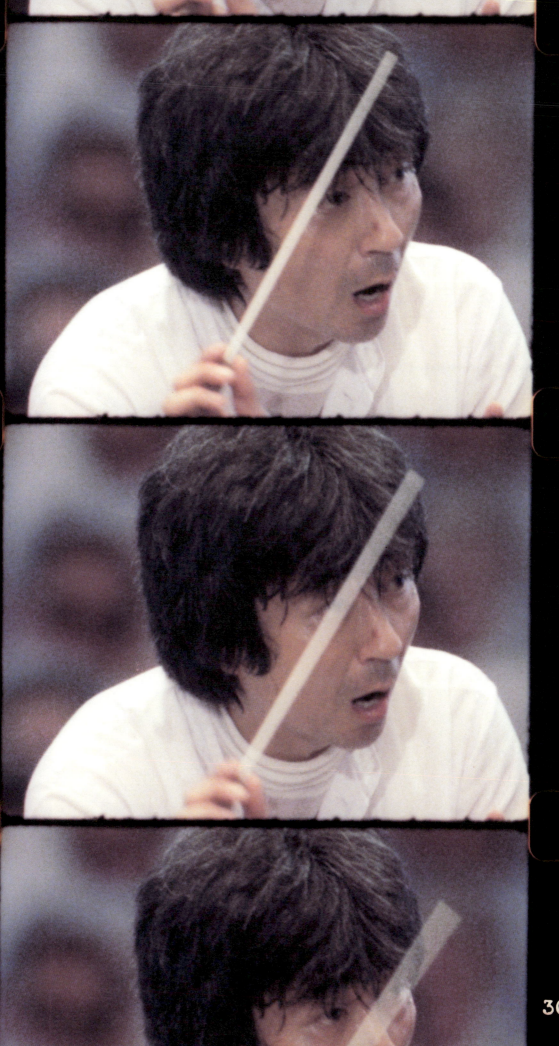

309

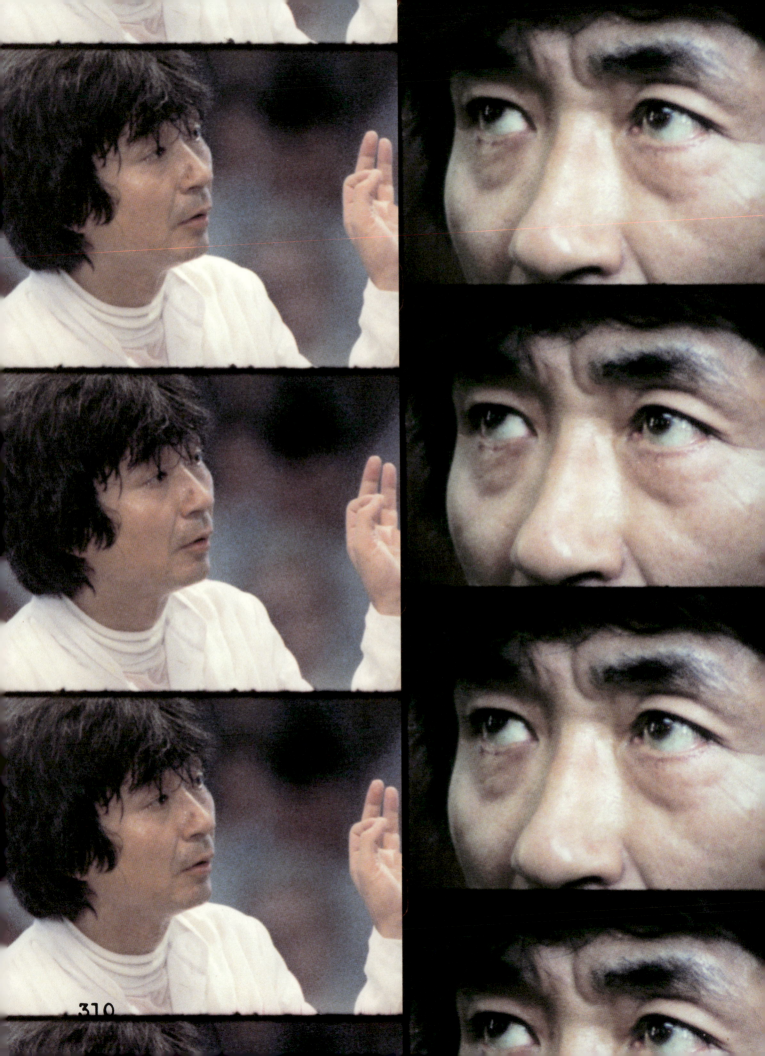

Christo's ISLANDS

islands 1986

A film that goes far beyond art, IS-LANDS celebrates the Bulgarian-born artist's ongoing fusion of culture, environment and politics. Since the late 1950's, Christo's large-scale temporary works of art have helped change our perception of art and society. In 1962, when the Maysles Brothers first met him in Paris, they immediately recognized a kindred spirit. As David Maysles said, "Christo comes up with an idea that at first seems impossible, then lets it grow; so do we." Albert Maysles agrees: "Both Christo's projects and our films are outrageous acts of faith."

The Maysles' first collaboration with Christo was VALLEY CURTAIN (1974), an Academy Award nominee. RUNNING FENCE followed in 1978. Then came ISLANDS. From Miami's Biscayne Bay on to Paris and Berlin, this film resonates with political intrigue: Christo's fight for permission to surround eleven Biscayne Bay islands with 6.5 million square feet of bright pink fabric, interwoven with his struggle to wrap the Pont-Neuf in Paris and the Reichstag in Berlin. From raucous public debates to off-the-record discussions, we see seven years of the artist at work: probing, politicking, debating the meaning of art.

Then comes the reward: Christo's first view from the air of his completed Islands. Art history in the making.

57 minutes, color
1986

From left: David and Albert Maysles, Charlotte Zwerin, Christo.

Photo: Gary Monroe

MAYSLES FILMS

From the 1960's on, Albert and David Maysles (along with such frequent co-filmmakers as Charlotte Zwerin, Susan Froemke and Ellen Hovde) have been making nonfiction feature films that are as compelling as fiction. Credited with the creation of "Direct Cinema" (the American cousin of the French *cinéma vérité*), the brothers have extended the boundaries of conventional documentaries—by filming real human dramas, by capturing life as it unfolds . . . without scripts, sets or narration.

Other Maysles films available on home video cassette include:

Salesman (1968)

Gimme Shelter (1970)

Christo's Valley Curtain (1974)

Grey Gardens (1976)

Running Fence (1978)

Ozawa (1985)

Vladimir Horowitz
The Last Romantic (1985)

Horowitz Plays Mozart (1987)

"A wryly funny and ultimately beautiful film. Splendid."
—*Bill Cosford, Film Critic, The Miami Herald.*

". . . captures the shimmering tropical poetry of blossoms more epic than any painted by Monet."
—*Manuela Hoelterhoff, Arts Editor, The Wall Street Journal.*

Maysles Films, Inc., 250 West 54th Street, New York, NY, 10019. (212) 582-6050

Islands

A MAYSLES FILMS, INC./C. ZWERIN PRODUCTION

Islands

Photo: Wolfgang Volz.

"Surrounded Islands," Biscayne Bay, Greater Miami, Florida, 1980-83, © Christo 1983.

Paris, Berlin, Miami. Three cultures, three Christo projects, reaching a crescendo in Biscayne Bay: eleven scrub-pine islands surrounded by 6.5 million square feet of bright pink floating fabric.

Christo: "This is my Monet *Water Lilies*."

A film by
Albert Maysles, Charlotte Zwerin and David Maysles

313

ISLANDS

-- Selected Quotes from the Film --

JEANNE-CLAUDE CHRISTO: You will never catch any person you know waking up his wife and kids early to go to a museum, saying "Let's go see if [the painting's] still there--" But that's what they'll do with Christo's Islands.

•••••••

CHRISTO: I always think of this as my most painterly project. It's like [making] gigantic paintings, each one of those islands is like a shaped canvas, like marvelous water lilies. It's my Claude Monet "Water Lilies"...

•••••••

REPORTER: While your work is no doubt appreciated, how do you respond to the average citizen in Miami who says you are going to do <u>what</u>? And it's going to be <u>where</u>? Are you kidding?

CHRISTO: That's probably your question, no? (*Laughter.*)

REPORTER: Well... Sort of.

•••••••

COUNTY COMMISSIONER RUVIN: I... I can't overcome my own personal feeling that your Biscayne Bay project is conceptually offensive. It is exploitive of something that I regard as beautiful, as sacrosanct in its natural form.

•••••••

CHRISTO: The very bottom of it is: "<u>Is it art?</u>" The commissioners are very upset, very uneasy that [my work] is considered art. If it were a back-drop for some multi-million-dollar Hollywood production, there would be no problem. They would burn the islands!

•••••••

COUNTY COMMISSIONER VALDEZ: I would like to know how much money the artist is going to have to invest in this project?

CHRISTO: A million and a half dollars.

VALDEZ: Beg your pardon?

CHRISTO: Million and a half dollars.

VALDEZ: And how much are the projected profits?

CHRISTO: There aren't any.

(*Silence.*)

Maysles Films is pleased to announce

HOROWITZ
PLAYS
MOZART

has been selected to premiere at

The 25th New York Film Festival

◆　　◆　　◆

A Peter Gelb production of a
new Maysles film by
Albert Maysles, Susan Froemke and Charlotte Zwerin

Thursday, October 8, 1987 at 6:15pm

**Alice Tully Hall
Lincoln Center, New York City**

Photo. A scene from the film "Horowitz Plays Mozart"

316

HOROWITZ: BACH

HOROWITZ: MOZART

HOROWITZ: SCHUBERT

HOROWITZ: SCHUMAN

HOROWITZ: CHOPIN

CAMI VIDEO presents
a PETER GELB/MAYSLES FILMS-FROEMKE co-production

SOLDIERS OF MUSIC

ROSTROPOVICH RETURNS TO RUSSIA

"We never said what wasn't true."
— Mstislav Rostropovich upon his return to the Soviet Union after a 16 year exile.

An extraordinary journey by a renowned and once-condemned artist to his former home—a home that stripped him of his citizenship, but is now welcoming him back; a home in which the old rules no longer apply, but a new order does not yet exist. A film about art, courage and conscience.

A film by
Susan Froemke, Peter Gelb, Albert Maysles, Bob Eisenhardt

National PBS Premiere: Jan. 1, 1991, 9:30 pm EST
(check local PBS listings for station information)
NEW YORK PREMIERE: Jan. 2, 1991, 9:30 pm, WNET-13

Maysles Films, Inc., 250 West 54th Street, New York, NY 10019 (212) 582-6050

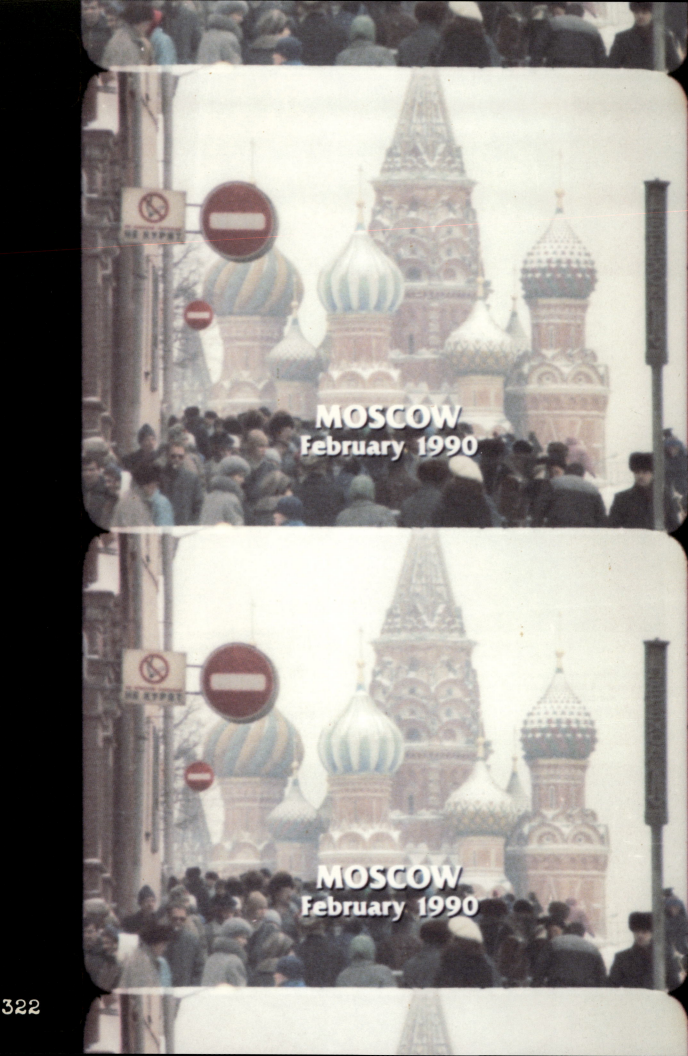

322

323

324

2624

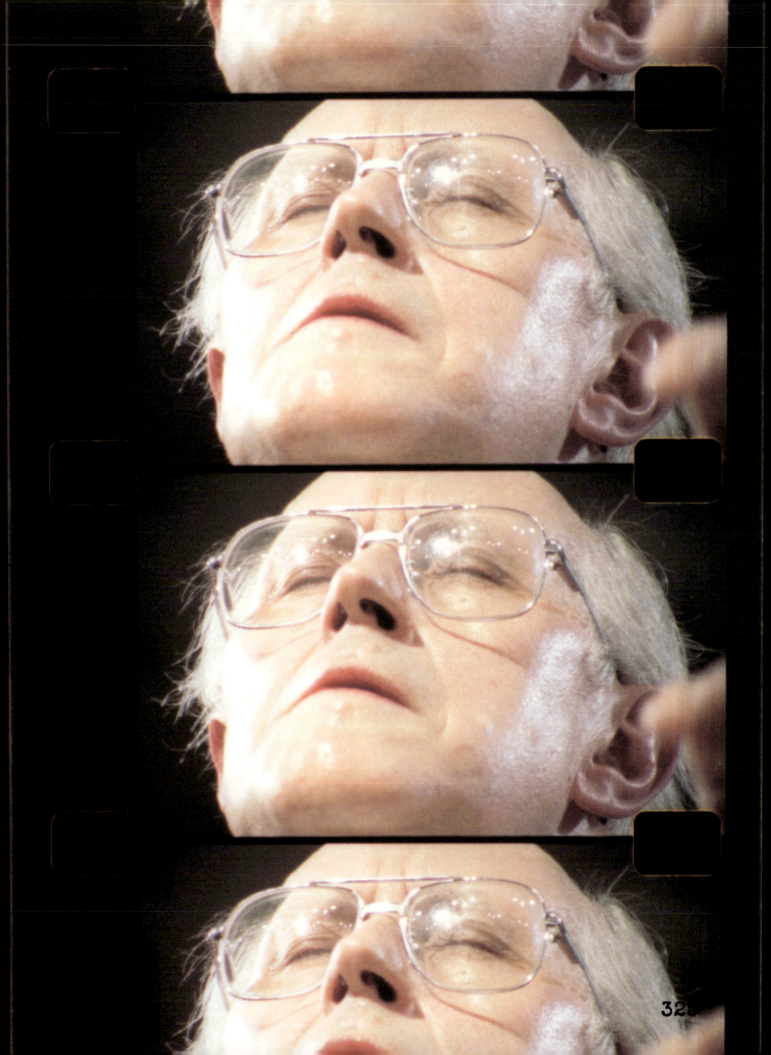

326

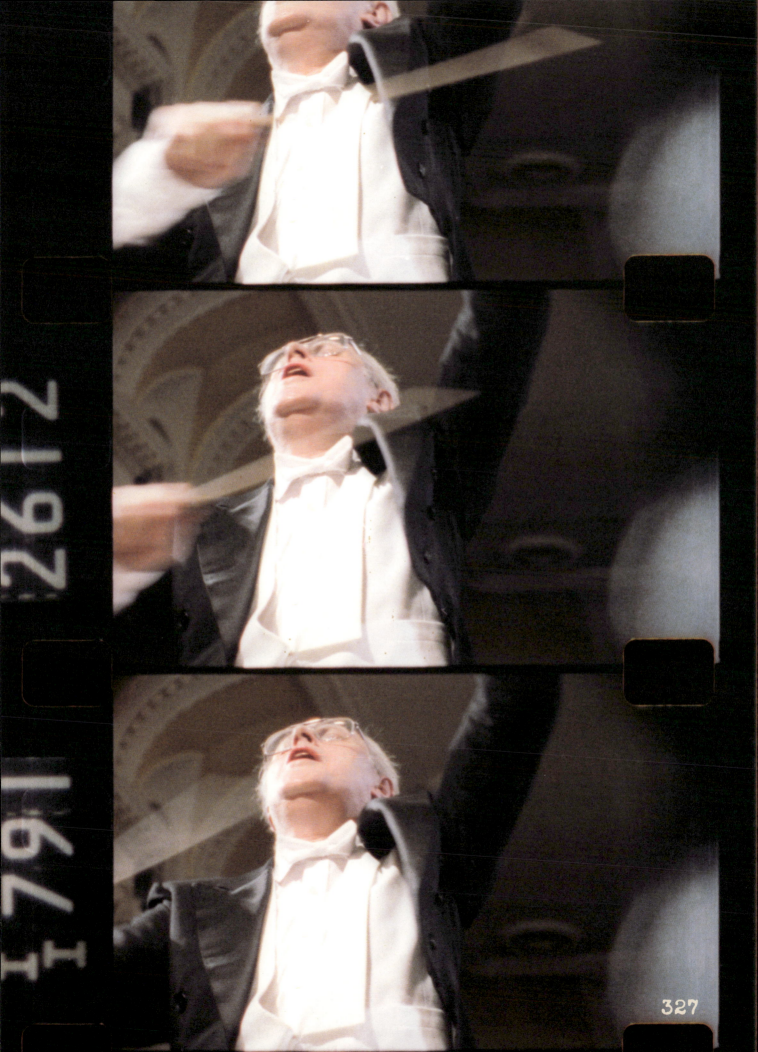

327

"My neighbor had inserted a wire hanger into her womb in order to abort. She then crawled six feet to the bathroom and that's where they found her—dead—in a puddle of blood... And this was an intelligent woman." Christina, 19

Melissa: All I'm doing is removing tissue from my body right now and an egg that's multiplying. That's it—it's nothing
Mom: But it is—
Melissa: It's not formed, it's not even starting to form.
Mom: Well, that's how you started out.

Mother and daughter, 1991

328

From *ABORTION: Desperate Choices*
A film by Susan Froemke and Deborah Dickson, with Albert Maysles
An HBO release of a Maysles Films, Inc. production

"My mother got pregnant again and she didn't want another child. So she took something my father got at the drugstore and she hemorrhaged. She was rushed to the hospital. Finally father came home — we were three little girls — and he said your mother's not coming home — she's gone to heaven." Hazel, 1924

"It's hard because we're already talking in the past tense — but it's still present. It 'would have been the baby' this and that, but now it's kinda hard because in a matter of minutes the baby's not going to be there."
Christine and Dan (moments before abortion), 1991

From *ABORTION: Desperate Choices*
A film by Susan Froemke and Deborah Dickson, with Albert Maysles
An HBO release of a Maysles Films, Inc. production

329

2

331

332

333

Christo : The Umbrellas
(Joint project For Japan and USA)

クリスト　アンブレラ、日本とアメリカ合衆国のためのジョイント・プロジェクト

MAYSLES FILMS, INC.
250 W. 54th St.
NYC 10019
212-582-6050

Left to right: The artist Christo and filmmakers Albert Maysles and Henry Corra on location for <u>The Umbrellas</u> in California.

Christo : The Umbrellas

For thirty years internationally renowned filmakers Albert Maysles and his late brother David, along with his co-filmmakers at Maysles Films have been recognized as the leading exponents of the non-fiction feature documentary. Their work includes such classics as <u>Salesman</u> (1968), <u>Gimme Shelter</u> (1970), and <u>Grey Gardens</u> (1976). The filmmakers have already collaborated with the environmental artist Christo on three heralded films: <u>Valley Curtain</u> (1974), nominated for an Academy Award; <u>Running Fence</u> (1978), praised by the New York Times as "the next best thing to having been there; " and, most recently, <u>Christo in Paris</u> (1990), the artist's audacious wrapping of the oldest, most celebrated bridge in Paris.

It is now Albert Maysles' intention with his co-filmmaker Henry Corra to complete a film about Christo's latest art work, <u>The Umbrellas, Joint Project for Japan and U.S.A.</u> Drawn from many hours of exclusive footage--shot over the past 5 years, during Christo's relentless struggle to realize his <u>Umbrellas</u> project--this 16mm documentary will be approximately ninety minutes in length.

337

338

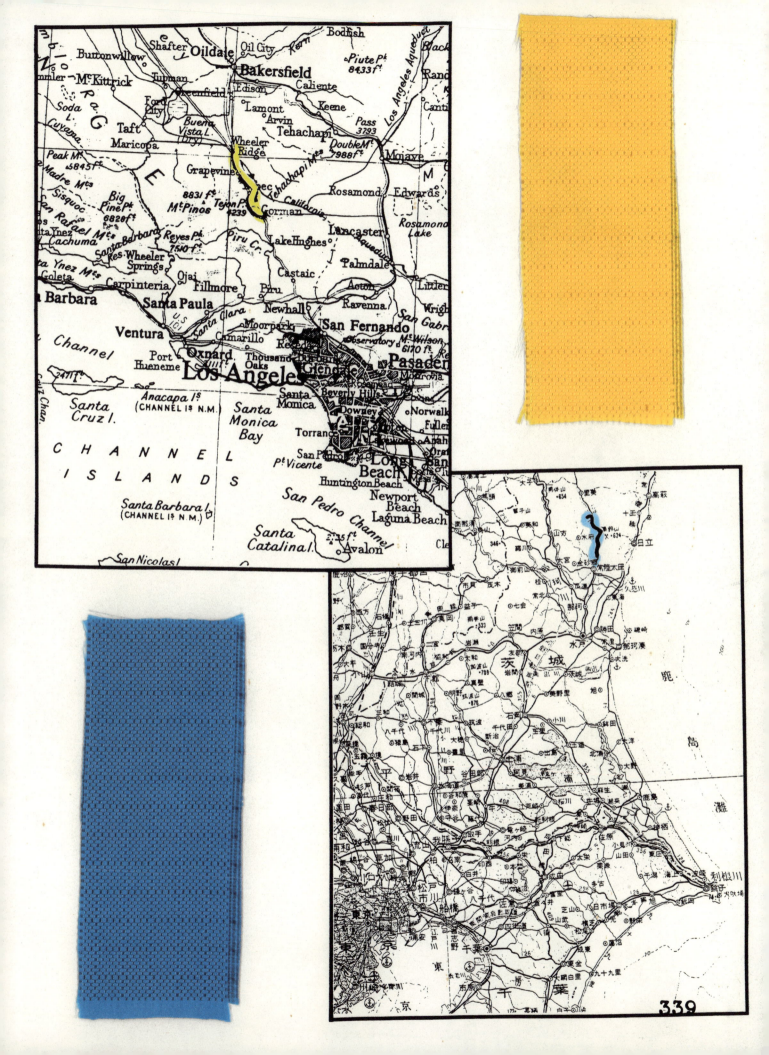

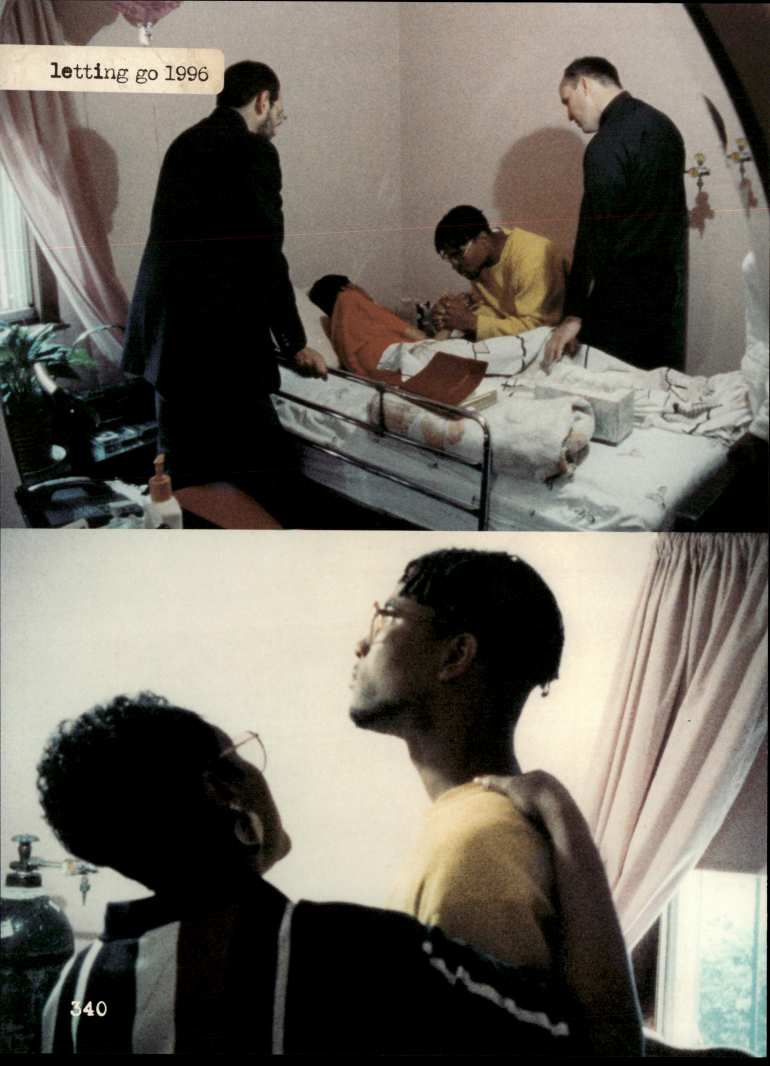

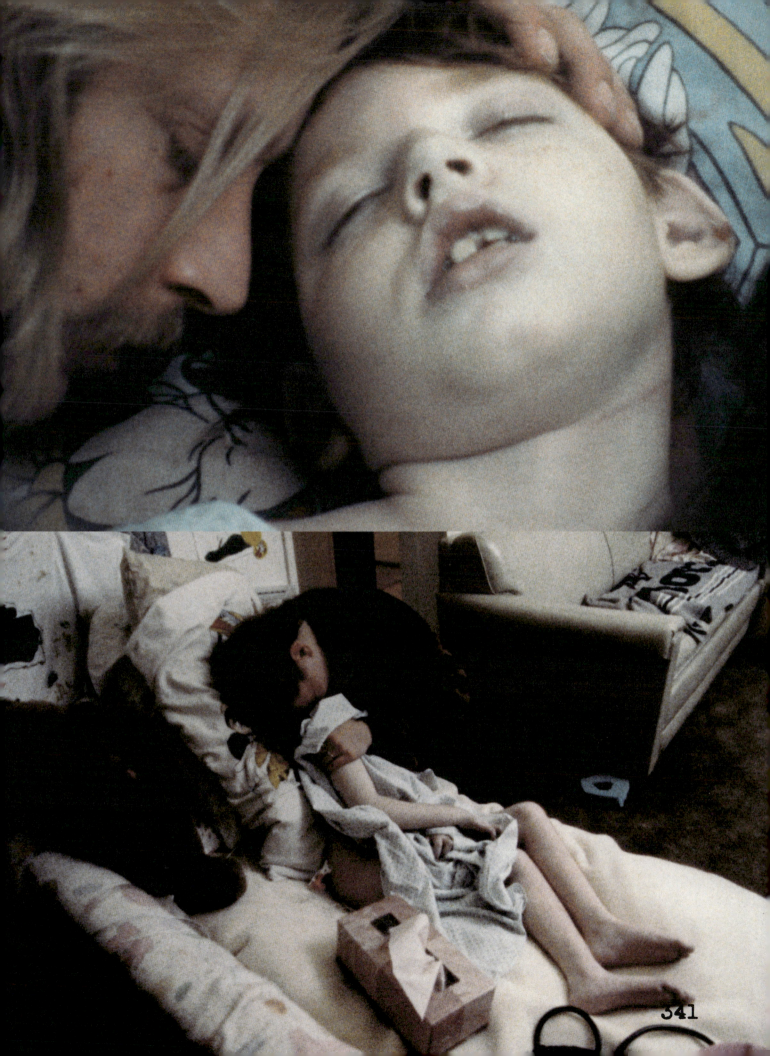

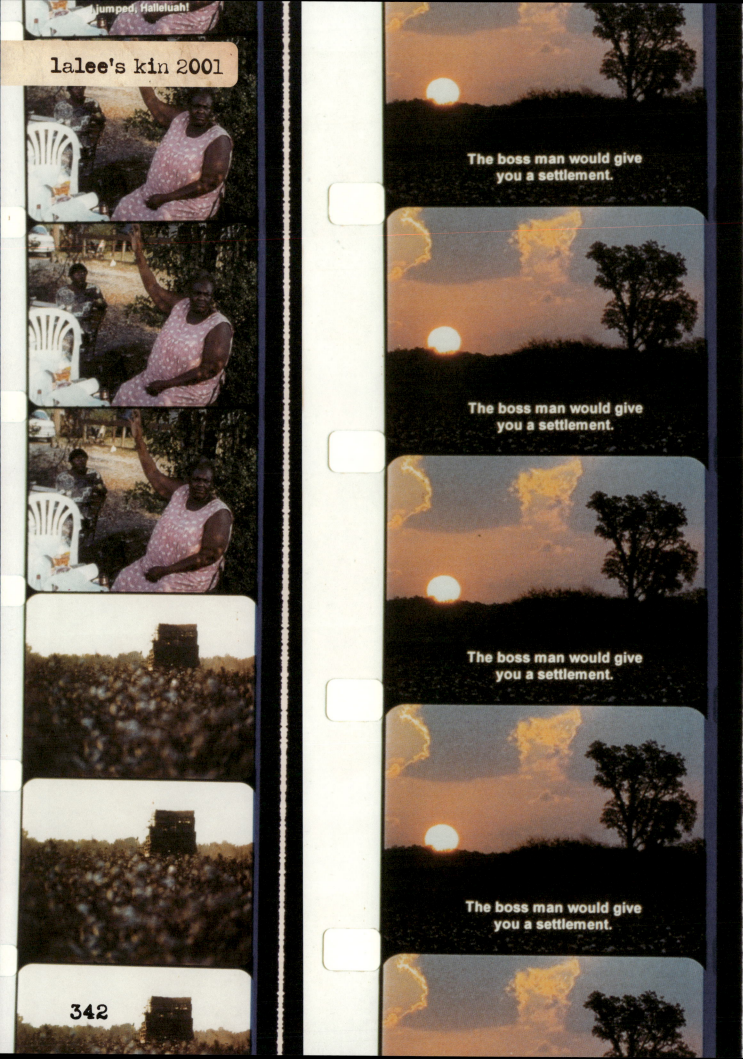

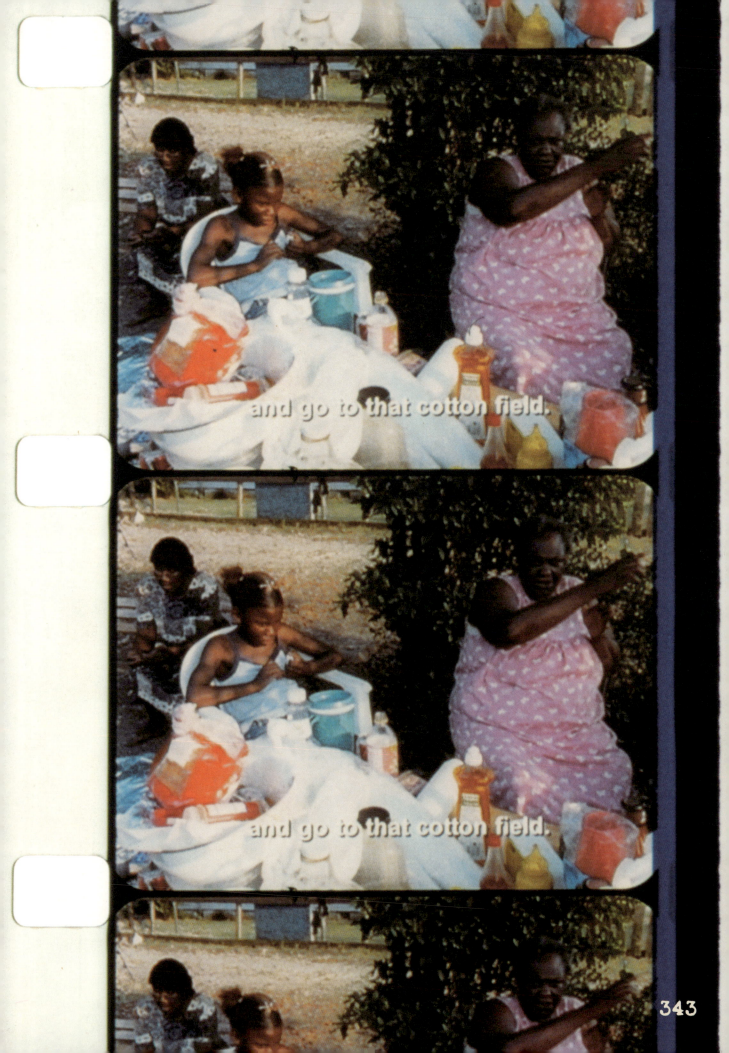

and go to that cotton field.

and go to that cotton field.

343

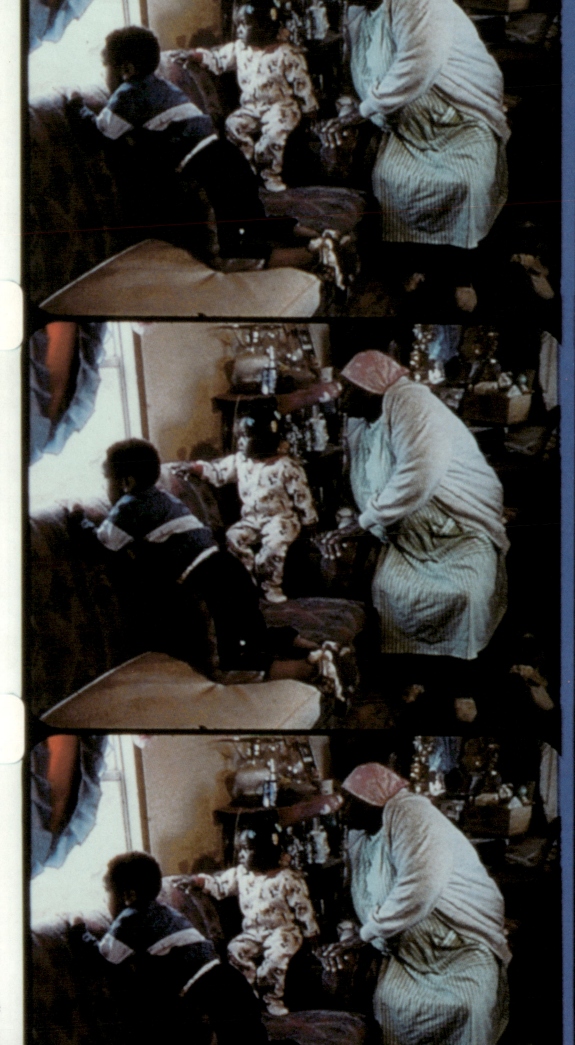

That's what I get a month.

That's what I get a month.

That's what I get a month.

That's what I get a month.

345

That's what I get a month.

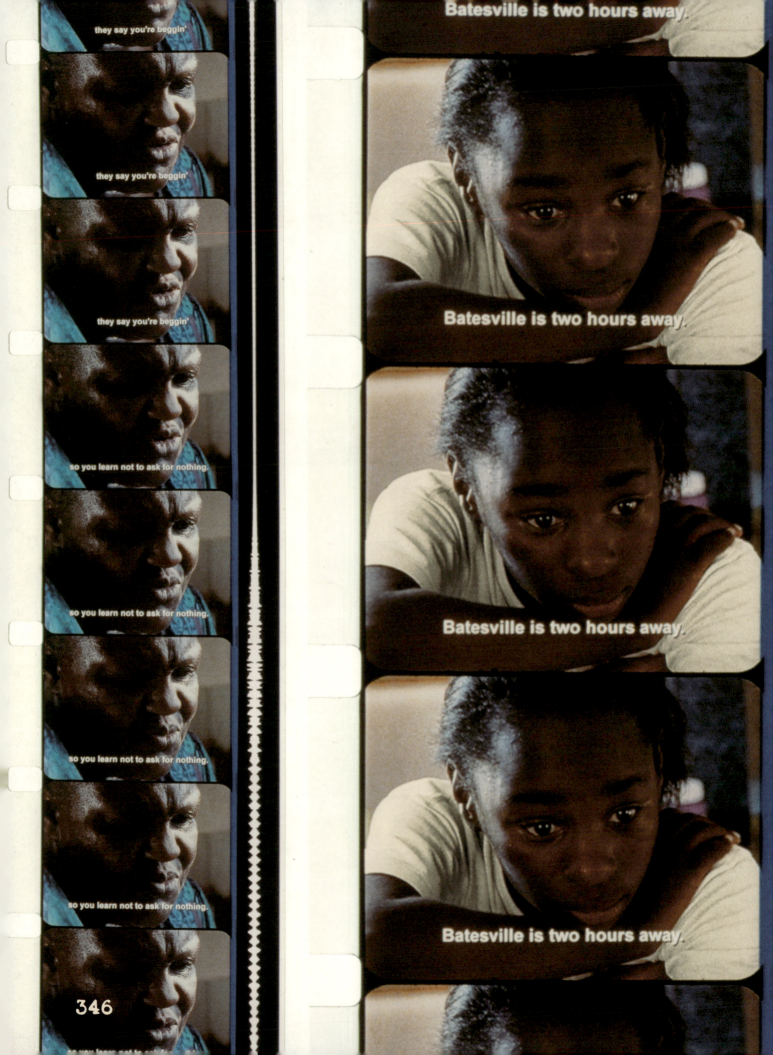

We was 11 boys and 12 girls, us.

We was 11 boys and 12 girls, us.

347

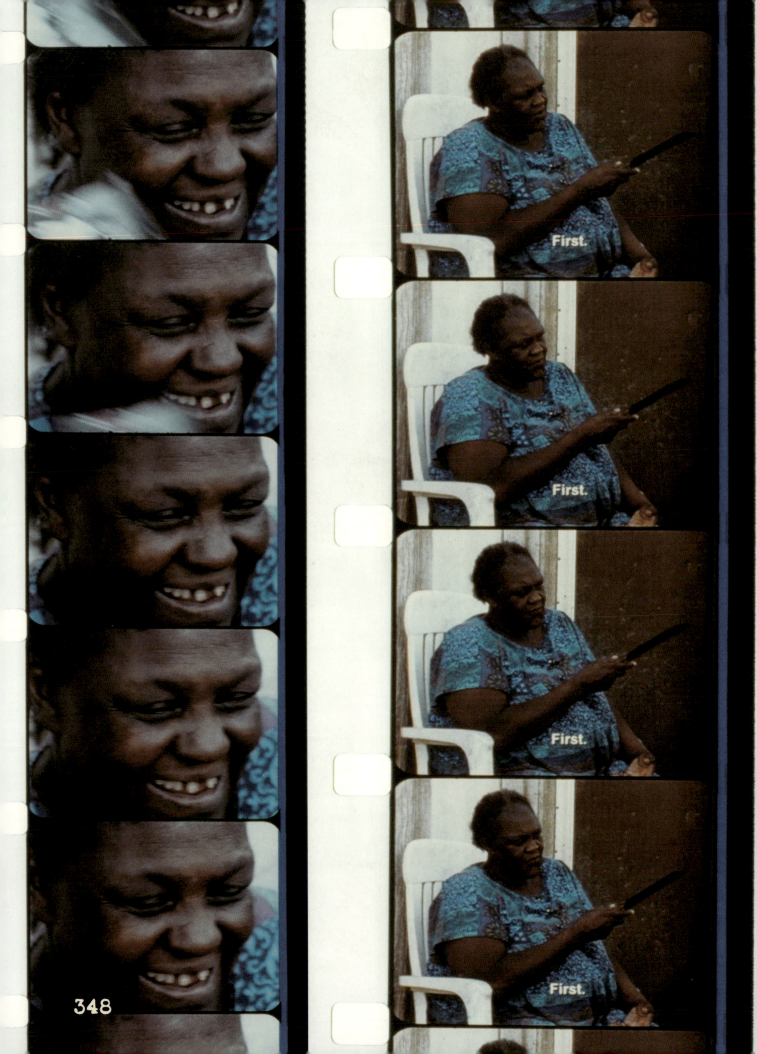

348

First.

First.

First.

First.

351

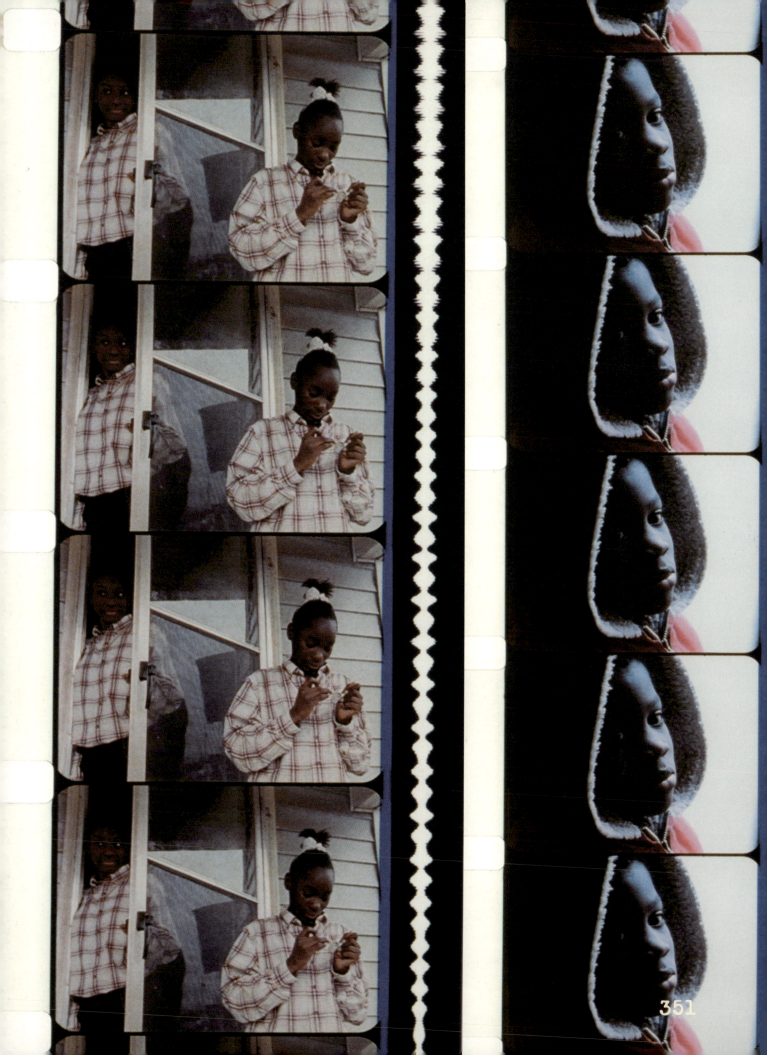

351

353

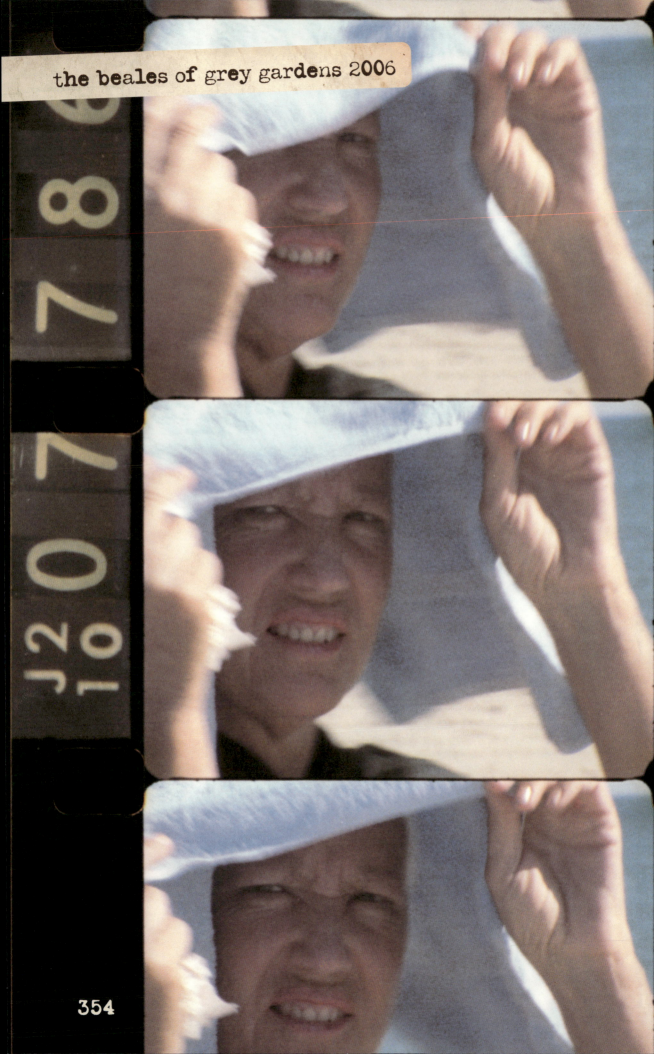

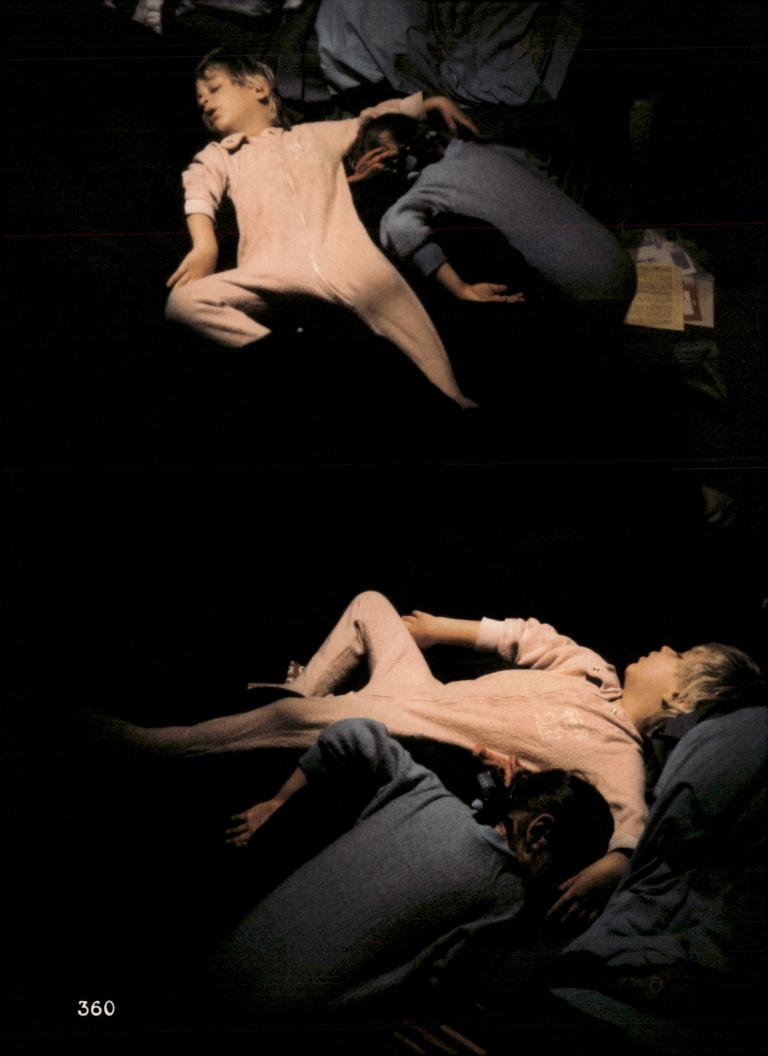

1, David Maysles at 8 years old, asleep. Photograph by Albert Maysles, aged 12 years old, circa 1939.

2, David Maysles taking a light meter reading for the film *Mother*, 1968.

3, Charlotte Zwerin, editor and co-filmmaker of many Maysles productions, takes a light meter reading for the film *Mother*, 1968.

4 - 5, David and Albert Maysles with film equipment in New York City, promoting the film *Salesman*, circa 1968. Photograph by Tony Anthony.

6, Film canisters and containers in the Maysles Films Archive's cold storage, 2007. Photograph by Kristine Larsen.

8 - 9, All the equipment needed for a film crew of two, including Albert Maysles' customized 16mm camera and David Maysles' Nagra sound recorder. Photographer unknown.

10 - 11, Albert's 16mm camera and David Maysles' Nagra sound recorder with a detailed breakdown of the specs of both.

12 - 13, Albert and David Maysles in Germany where David was stationed in the army, after Al took a motorcycle journey through Europe, 1954. Photographer unknown.

14 - 15, Albert in the National Hotel, Moscow, 1956. Photograph by Elena Bekhterova.

16 - 17, Albert behind his custom engineered 16mm camera. Photographer unknown.

18 - 19, David, a nurse, and Albert stuck in a hospital after Al broke his leg riding on top of a car he hailed down so that David could pick up a girl on their motorcycle. Poland, 1957. Photographer unknown.

20, David and Albert in front of the Kremlin, on the motorcycle they drove through Russia and Poland in 1957. Photographer unknown.

22, Autobiography of Albert Maysles written to prospective sponsors of a 1956 trip to Eastern Europe. Note the typo: June 15, 1965 should be June 15, 1956.

23, Albert on return from Russia wearing a Russian hat, Kufaika, and Ukrainian shirt. Photographer unknown.

24, Notes for "Russian Close-Up" lecture. Includes contact prints of photographs by Albert Maysles, 1955.

25 - 31, Photographs by Albert from his first trip to the Soviet Union, taken with a Leica 35mm camera. The captions that follow were written at the time by Albert, excepting a few additional comments.

25, Girl at gate, photographed in a Moscow suburb.

26, top: Metro Talk. Moscow subway.

26, bottom: Subway Thinking. I saw the familiar sight of people reading books such as Maupassant, Gorki, or even Mark Twain. Others carried with quiet dignity the same vacant stare of subway passengers the world over.

27, top: Something's Funny. It is Sunday and people on this street are walking to the park. The accordion player is playing for the fun of it.

27, bottom: Somewhat Suspicious. Moscow street scene.

28, top: Zagorsk is a Religious Center: Last year this town (Zagorsk, 45 miles from Moscow) celebrated its 600th anniversary. It has 6 churches and a seminary. Services are held all day. This church is open from 5am to 7pm.

28, bottom: Boat station on Moscow River.

29, top: Muscles at the Stalin Auto Works. About 60% of the machinery in this part of the plant carried trade names of English, German, and American companies. The Stalin Auto works employs 40,000 workers.

29, bottom: Round Rims. At the Stalin Auto Works this girl is putting together bicycle wheels. Bicycles will retail at 600 rubles ($150 at the American rate of exchange).

30, top: Folk Dance. Girls dance together at the park.

30, bottom: Putting on the Hex—Moscow Style. Putting on a little show for the cameraman, these Moscow children are making the "hex" above the central figure. This game, quite common in this country, was not prompted by the American cameraman; it came spontaneously from the children. Apparently it is a Russian as well as an American custom. It is interesting to note the similarity between this sign and the "v" for victory gesture. Behind the boys is a Russian made Pobeda.

31, top: Architect and Draftsman.

31, bottom: Three on a Rope. These children are playing jump-rope in back of their new apartment house in suburban Moscow.

32 - 33, Prospectus for "Russia Close-Up" lecture and film presentation, 1956.

34 - 35, Scene from Albert's first 16mm film, *Russian Close-Up*, 1956. Albert's caption: These women were plaintiffs in the Moscow City Court. They came to complain that the job to which they had been transferred paid only half as much as they had been getting. They were reinstated. A moment after this picture was made, the woman in the center turned to the one nearest the camera and complained that she thought she had talked too much. This woman then replied, "What do you mean talk too much... I can say what I want to say... this is a free country... This is the Soviet Union, not the United States of America." Immediately behind them stands Prof. Harold Berman, Harvard authority on Soviet Law.

36 - 37, Flyer for lecture and film presentation of *Russian Close-Up* and *Mental Health in Russia*, 1959.

38, Albert Maysles with psychiatrists (in white) and patients at the Pavlov Psychiatric Hospital, Kiev. Behind them a bust of Pavlov. "I soon discovered that Soviet application of Pavlovian theory does not emphasize social causes as the source of mental disturbance" 1956. Photographer unknown.

39, Article from local Boston newspaper, by Leo Shapiro, 1956.

40 - 43, Article from *MD* magazine, November, 1958.

44 - 51, Photographs by Albert for the lecture "Mental Health in Russia", 1955-56.

44, top: Psychiatrist and Patient. Dr. Patapova (right) is a psychiatrist and the assistant director of the Stalin Region Hospital #8 in Moscow. Here she is shown talking to a patient in the gardens built by the hospital patients.

44, bottom: Nurse and patient listen to a record on hospital grounds at Stalin Region Hospital #8 in Moscow.

45, top: This ward, with four beds on each side, and bare walls was typical of those seen. Here at Stalin Region Hospital #8 in Moscow, as in the other two hospitals visited, patients are moved from ward according to stage of recovery. There were five such stages at this hospital.

45, bottom: This patient at the Stalin Region Hospital #8 in Moscow is receiving Thorazine for sleep therapy. Injections of this drug will keep the patient asleep for about 15 hours. Drug and electric sleep therapy appeal to the Russian psychiatrists partly because of their emphasis on the physical rather than the mental basis of nervous disorder. From left to right are patient, psychiatric nurse, and psychiatrist (Dr. Mejaskaia).

46 - 47, At right a Red Army lieutenant suffering from attacks of anxiety and diagnosed as neurosthenic is undergoing electro-sleep therapy at Stalin Region Hospital #8 in Moscow. At left is psychiatrist Dr. Sehavanova, who has regulated the apparatus on the table so that a small amount of alternating current will keep the patient asleep for about an hour after which he will continue to sleep for two or three more hours. The patient works as an army officer during the day and attends the Institute for Radio evenings. Psychiatrist Dr. Meyaskaia said he was ill from overwork. Family problems were ruled out (a happy home life, married and one child). Two negative electrodes have been placed over the eyelids (the eyes are considered by the Russians to give better conduction). Two negative electrodes have been placed just below and in the back of the ears. This apparatus was first used in this hospital in 1950. Note that this is electric-sleep therapy and not electric shock, which is considered by the Russians to be a brutal form of therapy and is used only when all other methods of treatment fail.

48, top: Patients and some of the staff at the Pavlov Psychiatric Hospital in Kiev.

48, bottom: Patients and psychiatrists (in white) at the Pavlov Psychiatric Hospital in Kiev.

49, "Stringer" for CBS and Baltimore Afro-American Journalist William Worthy takes notes on a patient at a Russian mental hospital 1955. It was due to William Worthy that Albert was able to sneak into a reception at the Rumanian Embassy in Moscow, an event which provided the connections he needed to gain permission to visit and film in Russian mental hospitals. Present were journalists, U.S. Government officials and key players in the Russian government at the time—Lazar M. Kaganovich, Anastas I. Mikoyan, Mikhail G. Pervukhin, Mikhail A. Suslov and Georgi M. Malenkov.

50, top: Ward room typical of those seen in USSR.

50, bottom: 12 year-old girl in classroom for emotionally disturbed children, Soloviev mental hospital in Moscow.

51, Patient at Pavlov Psychiatric Hospital, Kiev.

52, "It's not cultured," Marguerite Drozdovitch, age 18. "It's not cultured," she says, as I wink at her in taking the photograph. (Now Al tells a different story: Insisting on accompanying Marguerite, his girlfriend at the time, to her small hometown, she wagged her finger to remind Al, once again, that he couldn't get off the train with her. It was prohibited for foreign visitors to visit small towns like hers, part of strict Russian government policies on foreigners traveling in the USSR, which Al often ignored.)

53, Outside train station, Moscow.

54, top: Moscow school children, first week of school. School begins September. Russian children start school at 7 years old.

54, bottom: Moscow school children.

55, I could not communicate with this Tatar from east central Russia except by staring—he looked at West and I at East. Under his hat, a skull cap as is worn in Tataria.

56, Waiting room, Moscow Airport. Peasant woman waits for plane.

57, Girl awaits plane, Moscow Airport.

58 - 59, It's softer this way! A heap of people sleep in an anteroom at Moscow Airport at dawn. It's softer this way. The family here, sleeping on baggage and each other, is waiting overnight for a plane in Moscow's airport. Scenes like this are more common in railway depots where people must often wait several days to get on over-crowded trains.

60, top and bottom: In Prague I appeared on television, on a 15-minute program entitled "A Scooterist on a Scooter." The program began with my riding the scooter from the street into the studio. Here I am telling the television audience the story of my trip. I got paid 500 crowns (at 7 to the dollar), with 20 taken out for Czech income tax. It paid my expenses for my remaining four days in Czechoslovakia. As I left Prague the next day hundreds of people reached forward to shake my hand—they had seen me on television the night before. As one commented on the excitement of the others, "People here are crazy for Americans."

61, top: I passed out cherries to children I met along the way.

61, bottom: Children ran after the scooter — something entirely new to them — as I rolled through Eastern Czechoslovakia 60 miles from the Russian border.

62, Beer and Gas. On the road to Jhlava, in Western Czechoslovakia, truckmen stopped to talk. I accepted their offer—as much beer as I could drink and as much gas as a scooter would hold. Photograph by Daphne Adams.

63, top: Albert traveling by motorscooter through Italy, Austria, Yugoslavia, Czechoslovakia, Poland, and Russia, 1956.

63, bottom: Gathering the harvest—Eastern Czechoslovakia.

64 - 65, Photographs for *Polish Youth*, 1957.

64, Polish youth picking up brick to hurl at militiamen, Warsaw, Poland on second night of student demonstrations against banning of student paper "Po Postu" last October.

65, Article and photograph from *Life* magazine on Polish demonstrations.

66 - 67, Albert and David interviewing for *Youth in Poland*, 1957.

68 - 85, Photographs by Albert in collaboration with Charles Dee Sharp for book (never published) and film, *On the Path of Paul*, alternately titled *Journey of St. Paul*. Captions primarily by Sharp.

68 - 69, An Anatolian farmer corrals his cows.

70, Letter from Albert to David Maysles.

71, Turkish boy watches passing train.

72, "So faith hope love abide, these three; but the greatest of these is love."

73, top: Al with Leica, Mt. Ararat behind. Photograph by Charles Dee Sharp.

73, bottom: Map of journey through Turkey.

74, top: A girl with donkey, Philippi, Turkey.

74, bottom: Young Turkish girls at play.

75, top and bottom: Turks greeting a passing train.

76 - 77, "Love is patient and kind; love is not jealous or boastful; it is not arrogant or rude. Love bears all things, believes all things, believes all things, endures all things."

78 - 79, Eskisehir bound train, Turkey.

80, top: In Tarsus, Paul's birthplace, I saw hundreds of small shops where men worked with "their own hands." The July sun is hot, indeed, and these shoemakers begin their work at 5:30 in the morning. They rest in the afternoon and work again until 9 or 10 o'clock in the evening.

80, bottom: The rich vineyards in Western Anatolia produce the sultana grape. This grape is sweet, seedless; to my mind the best tasting in the world. "Be not deceived;" Paul wrote to the Galatians, "God is not mocked: for whatsoever a man soweth, that shall he also reap. And let us not be weary in well doing: for in due season we shall reap, if we faint not."

81, top: Not far from Trouva, or ancient Troy, on the way to Alexandria Troas where the Dardanelles join the Aegean Sea, I met these gypsy boys. In the bright heat the bears were incongruous and ironical looking, though tame. Seeing me, a bearded stranger, but in their eyes an obvious tourist, they stopped, and began rattling their tambourines. The bears, even without being pulled, raised to their hind legs and began to gyrate. The boys asked for money. "If I speak in the tongues of men and of angels but have not love I am a noisy gong or a clanging symbol."

81, bottom: Beggars greet a passing train.

82 - 83, Beggar and young girl on a street in Istanbul.

84, top and bottom: A Turkish village's water supply.

85, The first page of a longer article in Modern Photography about *On the Path of Paul*, featuring Albert's photographs.

86 - 95, Photographs by Albert, USSR 1959. No extant captions.

96 - 97, From unused footage, 1959. This is some of the first film Albert shot on trains. Since then he has filmed passengers on trains throughout the world, to be compiled in the upcoming feature *In Transit*.

98 - 101, From Robert Drew's *Primary*, 1960. Along with other films produced by Robert Drew, this film was pivotal in the American Direct Cinema movement, with cinematography by Al, Richard Leacock, D.A. Pennebaker and Terrence McCartney-Filgate.

These cinemagraphs are representative of some of Al's work on the film.

98, Jackie Kennedy and John F. Kennedy at a rally during Kennedy's primary campaign against Humphrey in Wisconsin.

99, A fish-eye lens captures John F. Kennedy greeting his supporters at a primary rally.

100, John F. Kennedy greeting supporters.

101, Jackie Kennedy's hands.

102, Article on the film *Yanki, No!* from Cuban newspaper *Bohemia*, January 22, 1961.

103, Article from *Time* magazine, December 19, 1960.

104 - 105, From Robert Drew's *Yanki, No!*, 1961. Albert filmed this segment in which a Cuban family moves their meager belongings from their decrepit family shack into a brand new home built by the Cuban government.

106 - 107, From untitled footage from Albert's second trip to Cuba, 1961.

108, Al filming for the Drew Associates' *Kenya*, 1961.

109 - 113, From *Safari Ya Gari*, 1961. A short film of a train journey in Kenya. Shot contemporaneously with Drew Associates' *Kenya*. Cinematography by Albert Maysles. All images except those on page 113 are from outtake footage.

114 -115, From *Anastasia*, 1962. A short film following ballerina Anastasia Stevens, the only American dancer in the Bolshoi Ballet, as she prepares for a performance in New York. Cinematography by Albert Maysles.

116 - 123, From *Showman*, 1963. A 53-minute film about one of Hollywood's most prolific movie producers, Joseph E. Levine. *Showman* documents the life of Levine and the press hysteria surrounding *Two Women* (*La Ciociara*), 1960, starring Sophia Loren. Cinematography for *Showman* by Albert Maysles.

116, left: Joseph Levine with Sophia Loren's Best Actress Oscar for her work in *Two Women*, which he received on her behalf.

116, right: Joseph Levine with his housekeeper looking at Sophia Loren's Oscar.

117, left: Kim Novak. From *Showman* outtake footage.

117, right: Sophia Loren and Romy Schneider at Cannes.

118, Sophia Loren.

119, Joseph Levine, Sophia Loren.

120, top: Joseph Levine and Boston priests.

120, bottom: Joseph Levine, Sophia Loren.

121, top: Sophia Loren.

121, bottom: Joseph Levine, Sophia Loren.

122 - 123, Sophia Loren with Oscar.

124 - 129, Works for Hire 1964 - 1967.

124, Albert and David Maysles with Gena Rowlands, 1967. Photographer unknown.

125, Frank Sinatra with Al and David on the set of the film *Tony Rome*, 1967. Al and David had been commissioned to make a behind the scenes 'Tony Rome' featurette. Photographer unknown.

126, top: David Maysles, Janet Margolin and Al Maysles during the filming of *20ᵗʰ Century Fox Press Junket,* 1965. Photographer unknown.

126, bottom: Raquel Welch being interviewed by Rex Morgan, with Al Maysles on camera, David on sound, during the filming of *20ᵗʰ Century Fox Press Junket,* 1965. Photographer unknown.

127, top: Elia Kazan and Arthur Miller collaborating on *After the Fall* and being filmed by Albert Maysles for a television program entitled *Theater of Tomorrow*, 1963. Photographer unknown.

127, bottom: Albert Maysles, Jack Cardiff, and David Maysles while filming *Sean O' Casey: The Spirit of Ireland, AKA Young Cassidy*, 1965. Photographer unknown.

128, Albert, Jean Luc Godard, Barbet Schroeder and Joanna Shimkus on the set of *Paris vu par...*, segment *Montparnasse-Levallois*, 1965. Photographer unknown.

129, Nude photograph by Albert for *American Photographer*, never published. Part of a series of nudes Al shot from a loft in his New York City apartment in the 1960s.

130 - 137, From *What's Happening! The Beatles in the U.S.A*, 1964. A behind the scenes account of first days of the Beatles' arrival in the USA in February 1964. Cinematography by Albert Maysles.

130, Title card for *What's Happening! The Beatles in the U.S.A.*

131, The Beatles coming off plane from London, at Idlewild (now JFK) Airport, New York City.

132, left: Crowds greeting the Beatles upon arrival at Idlewild.

132, right: Fans seen from inside the car the Beatles took from the airport to their Manhattan hotel.

133, left: Paul McCartney, radio in hand, listening to Murray the K playing their music in honor of their arrival.

133, right: John Lennon.

134, George lying on a train overhead luggage rack, acting like a vampire for the benefit of the press, train passengers, and the other Beatles.

135, left and right: Murray the K dancing at the Peppermint Lounge.

136, left: Unnamed young women dancing at the Peppermint Lounge.

136, right: Close-up on one of the dancing women.

137, Ringo on a photo shoot.

138 - 139, Albert Maysles, unknown interviewer, David Maysles, and Marlon Brando

on Central Park West, NYC, shooting *Meet Marlon Brando*. Photographer unknown.

140 - 141, Article from *Esquire* magazine, February 1965.

142 - 149, From *Meet Marlon Brando*, 1965. The film covers a one-day marathon press junket composed of interviews with reporters from local TV stations across the U.S., for Brando's film *Morituri*, 1965. Filmed on Central Park West and at the Hampshire House hotel in New York City. Cinematography by Albert Maysles.

142, left: Marlon Brando.

142, center: Marlon Brando on Central Park West with an unknown woman with whom he has struck up a conversation.

142, right: Marlon Brando and Lois Leppart.

143, left and center: Rex Morgan and Marlon Brando.

143, right: Brando.

144, left: Brando. From outtake footage.

144, center, right: Brando.

145, left: Brando.

145, center and right: Mary Frann and Brando.

146, left and center: Michelle Metrinko, First Runner-up Miss USA 1964, with Brando.

146, right: Brando.

147, left and center: Brando.

147, right: Bill Gordon and Brando. From outtake footage. Both this image and Brando's use of the word "fuck" in a joke had to be excised from the film in order to avoid an "R" rating.

148 - 149, Bill Gordon and Brando.

150, top: Advertisement for NET television showing of *With Love from Truman*.

150, bottom: David, Truman Capote, Al. Photograph by Bruce Davidson.

151, top: David, Al, Truman Capote. Photograph by Bruce Davidson.

151, bottom: Al, David, Truman Capote. Photograph by Bruce Davidson.

152 - 153, From *With Love from Truman*, 1966. The film visited Truman Capote at his home in the Hamptons, just following publication of *In Cold Blood*. That groundbreaking "non-fiction novel" had parallels to David and Al's commitment to the "non-fiction feature film." All images from outtake footage. Cinematography Albert Maysles.

154 - 159, From *MGM Press Junket*, 1966. Cinematography by Albert Maysles.

154, Roman Polanski on the set of *The Fearless Vampire Killers*.

155 - 159, Sharon Tate and David Hemmings dancing together at an MGM Party.

160 - 165, From *Dali's Fantastic Dream*, 1966. A short that follows Dali as he creates a painting, part of promotion

for the film *Fantastic Voyage*. Cinematography by Albert Maysles.

160, Salvador Dali at a department store preparing to create.

161, Dali on a New York street outside the department store.

162 - 163, Part of Dali's creative process, styrofoam confetti rains down on Dali's head.

164, left: Salvador Dali with horn and wig, also part of his creative process, in front of painting.

164, right: In a department store, Dali directs his model, actress Raquel Welch.

165, Close-up on Dali.

166 - 167, Letter from David Maysles, written in 1966, to the South Western Company seeking subjects for the film *Salesman*.

168 - 169, Albert, David, Raymond Martos, Paul Brennan, and James Baker during the shooting of *Salesman*, 1967. Photograph by Bruce Davidson.

170 - 185, From *Salesman*, 1968. Cinematography by Albert Maysles.

170 - 171, The opening of the film, introducing Paul "The Badger" Brennan, James "The Rabbit" Baker, Raymond "The Bull" Martos, Charles "The Gipper" McDevitt.

172 - 173, Brennan in Florida.

174 - 176, Selling door to door in Florida.

177, Paul's hand on the Bible.

178 - 179, Making the pitch.

180, top: Brennan and Baker take a reprieve from work.

180, bottom: Ken Turner, sales manager of the Mid-American Bible Company, giving a speech at a national sales meeting at the Pleasant Valley Motor Lodge, Chicago, Ill.

181, top: Paul in the hotel room in Florida.

181, bottom: The salesmen play poker with sales manager Turner.

182 - 183, Paul waiting at the door of a potential customer, in the snow in Boston.

184 - 185, James Baker.

186, top: Albert and David, promo for *Salesman*, 1968. Photograph by Tony Anthony.

186, bottom: The four Bible salesmen, Paul Brennan, James Baker, Charles McDevitt, and Raymond Martos at the premiere of *Salesman*, 1968. Photograph by Bernard Gotfryd.

187, top: Albert and David promo for *Salesman*, 1968. Photograph by Bernard Gotfryd.

187, bottom: Paul Brennan, David, Al, and Raymond Martos look at reviews of *Salesman* at the premiere, 1968. Photograph by Bernard Gotfryd.

188 - 190, Ads for *Salesman*, 1968.

191, Congratulatory letter from the Mid-American Bible Company, 1969.

192 - 199, From *Mother*, an unfinished film shot in 1968. Al and David film their mother, Ethel Maysles as she gives a speech accepting the presidency to the local chapter of the National Jewish Congress, has Thanksgiving dinner with her children and grandchildren, and takes a train journey to her sons' New York offices. While explaining her life's philosophies, she praises her children and sweetly pushes them to get haircuts and, more importantly, get married. Cinematography by Albert Maysles.

192, David Maysles and Ethel Maysles on the train to New York City.

193, Ethel Maysles goes for a walk in the Maysles hometown of Brookline, Massachusetts.

194 - 195, Ethel Maysles at home in Brookline, Mass.

196, Ethel Maysles combs David's hair. David and Al's sister, Barbara Kramer sits in the background.

197, Ethel Maysles waves comb at Albert, behind the lens.

198, left: Charlotte Zwerin standing in for a light meter reading in the Maysles studio at 1697 Broadway, New York City.

198, right: Ethel Maysles at the studio, pointing to a still frame of Paul Brennan and James Baker from *Salesman*. Photographs of Raymond Martos and James Baker can also be seen as well as a photograph of Albert Maysles confined to a hospital bed in Poland, 1957.

199, Ethel Maysles in the editing rooms with editing assistant Barbara Jarvis.

200 - 235, *Gimme Shelter,* 1970. Chronicles a portion of the 1969 U.S. tour of The Rolling Stones that culminated in the fateful concert at the Altamont Speedway near San Francisco on December 6, 1969. Cinematography by Albert Maysles, Peter Adair, Baird Bryant, Joan Churchill, Ron Dorfman, Robert Elfstrom, Elliot Erwitt, Bob Fiori, Adam Giffard, William Kaplan, Kevin Keating, Stephen Lighthill, George Lucas, Jim Moody, Jack Newman, Pekke Niemela, Robert Primes, Eric Saarinen, Peter Smokler, Paul Ryan, Coulter Watt, Gary Weiss, Bill Yarhaus.

200 - 201, Charlie Watts. Photo shoot for the album cover of *Get Yer Ya Ya's Out! The Rolling Stones in Concert* (1970).

202 - 205, Mick Jagger at Madison Square Garden. The Rolling Stones were captured on film by the Maysles Brothers at Madison Square Garden on November 27ᵗʰ and at the afternoon and evening performances on November 28ᵗʰ, 1969.

206 - 207, Audience at Madison Square Garden.

208 - 210, *Gimme Shelter* outtake. Keith Richards in the studio during the mixdown sessions for *Get Yer Ya Ya's Out! The Rolling Stones in Concert.* London, 1970.

211, Keith Richards with Mick Jagger, Charlie Watts and Mick Taylor. Muscle Shoals, Alabama.

212 - 214, Tina Turner at Madison Square Garden. Ike and Tina Turner, B.B. King, Chuck Berry and Terry Reid supported The Rolling Stones

on several stops along the 1969 U.S. tour.

215, Tina Turner's Madison Square Garden performance captured on the Steenbeck editing console screen. London, 1970.

216 - 231, Altamont Speedway, Alameda County, California.

216, left: Unknown member of The Hell's Angels Motorcycle Club.

216, right: Construction of scaffolding the night before the free Altamont concert. December 5, 1969.

217 - 220, Concert attendees at Altamont Speedway.

221 - 223, Mick Jagger at the mic with an unknown member of the Hell's Angels Motorcycle Club.

224 - 225, Mick Jagger.

226 - 229, Jagger with an unknown audience member on stage at Altamont.

230, Unnamed concert attendees.

231, Meredith Hunter, center, photographed in the audience. Hunter was killed minutes later by Hell's Angels after Hunter was seen to brandish a gun.

232, left: *Gimme Shelter* outtake. Keith Richards and Mick Jagger mixing down *Get Yer Ya Ya's Out! The Rolling Stones in Concert.* London, 1970.

232, right: Charlie Watts, London, 1970.

233, Charlie Watts, Muscle Shoals studio, Alabama.

234, left: Steenbeck editing machine's screen showing Mick at Altamont. London, 1970.

234, right: Mick Jagger and David Maysles. London, 1970.

235, Mick Jagger.

236 - 237, Letter from David Maysles to Mick Jagger describing the proposed ending to *Gimme Shelter.*

238 - 241, Production notes on *Gimme Shelter* written by the Maysles brothers, published by *Filmmakers Newsletter* in December 1971.

242 - 243, David, Albert, and Charlotte Zwerin's response to Vincent Canby's article in the *New York Times,* "Making Murder Pay," 1970.

244 - 251, From *Grand Funk Railroad: Live at Shea Stadium,* 1971. A never-released concert film, made for TV. Cinematography by Albert Maysles and Richard Leacock.

244, Bassist Mel Schacher.

245, Crowds at Shea Stadium.

246 - 248, Drummer Don Brewer.

249, Guitarist and lead vocalist Mark Farner.

250, left: Don Brewer.

250, right: Mark Farner.

251, Mark Farner.

252, Cover of the VHS version of *Christo's Valley Curtain,* a film by David Maysles, Albert Maysles and Ellen Hovde.

253, Part of a press packet for *Christo's Valley Curtain.*

254 - 255, From *Christo's Valley Curtain,* 1973. One of six Maysles Films based on the art of Christo and Jeanne-Claude. Documents the construction of Christo and Jeanne-Claude's project entitled Valley Curtain, in Grand Hogback, Rifle, Colorado. Cinematography by Albert Maysles.

256 - 257, Postcard promoting the airing on Channel 13 of *The Burk Family of Georgia* AKA *The Burks of Georgia,* part of the *Six American Families* series. Photograph right by Marianne Barcellona.

258, From *The Burks of Georgia,* 1974. Documents three generations of an impoverished family struggling to live in Georgia. Cinematography by Albert Maysles.

259, Letter from Albert Maysles about the presentation of *The Burks of Georgia.*

260, Playbill from *Grey Gardens'* initial release in 1975 at the Paris Theatre, NYC.

261, From a press package mock-up for *Grey Gardens.*

262, From *Grey Gardens,* 1975, a complex portrait of mother and daughter, Edith "Big Edie" Bouvier Beale and Edith "Little Edie" Beale, Jr., aunt and cousin of Jackie Onassis. All cinematography in *Grey Gardens* by Albert Maysles. Here Al films himself and David in the Beales' East Hampton home.

263, Albert films himself and Little Edie Beale in a mirror of the Beales' bedroom.

264, The directors of *Grey Gardens*, David Maysles, Ellen Hovde, Albert Maysles, Muffie Meyer, and Susan Froemke. Photograph by Marianne Barcellona.

265, Albert and David with Big Edie and Little Edie during the shooting of *Grey Gardens*, 1973. Photograph by Albert Maysles.

266 - 267, Little Edie with David, 1973. Photograph by Albert.

268, Little Edie with scrap book. Photograph by Albert.

269, Little Edie with portrait of Big Edie as a young woman. From *Grey Gardens*.

270, Little Edie looking at phonograph record. From *Grey Gardens*.

271, Big Edie on the porch. Photograph by Albert.

272, top: Little Edie. Photograph by Albert.

272, bottom: Big Edie. Photograph by Albert.

273, top and bottom: Little Edie and Big Edie. Photograph by Albert.

274 - 275, Big Edie and Little Edie. Photograph by Albert Maysles.

276 - 286, Scenes from *Grey Gardens*.

287, Press pack quotes from *Grey Gardens*.

288 - 289, From transcript of *Grey Gardens*, Little Edie describing "the best outfit for today."

290 - 291, Little Edie and "The best outfit for today." From *Grey Gardens*.

292 - 293, Little Edie, Jerry "Marble Fawn" Torre and Big Edie. Photograph by Albert.

294 - 295, Scenes from *Grey Gardens*.

296 - 297, The final shots of *Grey Gardens*, Little Edie seen dancing through the banister of the staircase in the foyer.

298 - 299, Little Edie with Al's camera on her shoulder. Photograph by Albert.

300 - 301, Part of a press pack for *Running Fence*.

302 - 303, From *Running Fence*, 1978. Shot in Northern California, this film portrays Christo and Jeanne-Claude's endeavor to get permission to construct their project *Running Fence*, a 24-mile-long fence of white fabric. Cinematography by Albert Maysles.

304 - 307, From *Muhammad and Larry*, 1980. This film pays equal attention to former sparring partners Muhammad Ali and Larry Holmes as they prepare to fight each other for the World Heavyweight Championship. Cinematography by Albert Maysles.

304, Larry Holmes in training.

305, left: Larry Holmes.

305, right: Muhammad Ali. From outtake footage.

306, left: Ali in training. From outtake footage.

306, right: Ali in the ring with a sparring partner.

307, left: Muhammad Ali.

307, right: Another sparring match with Muhammad Ali.

308, From press pack for *Ozawa*, 1985.

309 - 311, From *Ozawa*, 1985. A portrait of conductor Seiji Ozawa behind the scenes and onstage at Tanglewood, Salzburg, Berlin and at home in Tokyo. The film captures Ozawa's personal struggle with the idea of being a Japanese man working in a Western musical tradition. Cinematography by Albert Maysles, Robert Leacock, Bob Richman.

312 - 313, *Islands* VHS tape cover.

314, Press pack quotes from *Islands*.

315, From *Islands*, 1986. Christo and Jeanne-Claude battle for permission to encircle eleven islands in Biscayne Bay, Miami with huge rings of pink fabric. Cinematography by Albert Maysles, Bob Richman, Erich Roland, Jeff Simon, Jeff Peterson.

316 - 317, Promotional material for *Vladimir Horowitz: the Last Romantic*, 1985, and *Horowitz Plays Mozart*, 1987. These are two intimate films about the pianist as he works and lives. The first is a portrait of Horowitz and his wife in their New York townhouse, the second follows Horowitz as he records works of Mozart, his first studio recordings in 35 years.

316, top: Postcard announcing the premiere of *Horowitz Plays Mozart* at the 25th New York Film Festival, 1987.

316, bottom: Albert filming Horowitz's hands on piano, while David captures sound, from the production of *Vladimir Horowitz: the Last Romantic*. Photograph by Larry Loewinger.

317, top: Still from *Horowitz Plays Mozart*, 1985. Cinematography by Albert Maysles, Vic Losick, Don Lenzer, George Bottos.

317, bottom: David and Albert Maysles in the editing studio during the production of *Horowitz Plays Mozart*. Photograph by Henry John Corra.

318 - 319, From *Christo in Paris*, 1990. In this film, as Christo and Jeanne-Claude prepare permissions for their latest project, the Pont Neuf, wrapped in beige fabric, they delve into their pasts and their ongoing love-affair with each other and the art they create. Cinematography by Albert Maysles, Don Lenzer, Bruce Perlman.

320, From *Soldiers of Music: Rostropovitch Returns to Russia*, 1991. In this film the conductor and cellist Mstislav Rostropovich returns home after 16 years of exile. Cinematography by Albert Maysles, Ed Lachman, Wolfgang Becker, Martin Schaer.

321, Postcard promoting the premiere of *Soldiers of Music* on PBS, 1991.

322 - 327, From *Soldiers of Music*.

328 - 329, Promotional material for *Abortion: Desperate Choices*.

330 - 333, From *Abortion: Desperate Choices*, 1992. This film explores both sides of the abortion controversy past and present, through first-person accounts, the activities of pro-life activists, and the experiences of women, their partners and relatives at the Women's Health Services Clinic in Pittsburgh. Cinematography by Albert Maysles, Bob Richman, Kenneth Love.

330, left: Pittsburgh pro-choice rally participants.

330, right: Carol reacting to a positive pregnancy test result in the counseling waiting room of the clinic.

331, left: Christine consoled by her boyfriend, Dan, after her abortion procedure.

331, right: Christine and Dan.

332, Laura, a pro-choice advocate, sings a psalm during a mass.

333, Melissa consoled by an abortion counselor following her abortion.

334 - 335, Cover and synopsis from a film proposal for *Umbrellas*, 1994.

336 - 338, From *Umbrellas*, 1994. Christo and Jeanne-Claude face the brute realities of the forces of nature in their attempt to erect large yellow umbrellas in California and blue umbrellas in a Japan in the midst of monsoon. Cinematography by Albert Maysles, Robert Richman, Gary Steele, Robert Leacock,

Don Lenzer, Richard Pearce, Martin Schaer.

339, Map with fabric samples from film proposal for *Umbrellas*.

340 - 341, From *Letting Go: A Hospice Journey*, 1996. The HBO film chronicles the struggles of three terminally ill hospice patients, their families, and the hospice workers who care for them, in their final months of life. Cinematography by Albert Maysles.

340, top: Hospice patient and cancer victim, 46 year-old Anna Turner with her son and priests on the day of her death, at her home in Queens, NYC.

340, bottom: Anna Turner's son receiving comfort from a hospice worker.

341, 8 year-old Michael Merseal Jr., a victim of brain disease with his father, Michael Merseal, in Missoula, Montana.

341, bottom: Michael and his estranged mother, reunited shortly before Michael's death.

342 - 353, From *Lalee's Kin: The Legacy of Cotton*, 2001, an intimate account of a life in poverty and of the problematic education system in Mississippi. Matriarch and great-grandmother Lalee Wallace, a onetime sharecropper, supports her complex extended family. Cinematography by Albert Maysles, Jim Dollarhide. A film by Susan Froemke, Deborah Dickson, Albert Maysles.

342, left: Lalee and a neighbor as they discuss the days when they used to work in the cotton fields, with a cut to an industrial cotton picker in a cotton field.

342, right: Sunset over cotton fields in Mississippi.

343, Lalee with her great-granddaughter, nick-named Granny, and a neighbor describing her days of work as a sharecropper.

344, Lalee and two of her great-grandchildren, Redman and Laura, wait in Lalee's trailer home for the arrival of a new trailer to house more of her family.

345, left: Lalee outside of her home with Redman and Main as she leads them through a song and prayer, "Touch me Jesus, touch my heart..."

345, right: Lalee as she discusses hard times trying to support her family and grandchildren on $494 a month.

346, left: Lalee talking about the sacrifices that must be made to live and support her family first.

346, right: Lalee's great-granddaughter, Cassandra (Granny) as Lalee describes why Granny lives with her and is sent to school while her mother works.

347, Granny and Lalee at home while Lalee talks about her childhood.

348, left: Lalee laughs as she watches her grandchildren and great-grandchildren play.

348, right: Lalee outside of her home as she discusses Main and Redman's poor schoolwork.

349, Two of Lalee's youngest grandchildren taking a bath in Lalee's plumbing-free trailer home.

350, Redman and two of his cousins take a bath using water collected in buckets from a city tap.

351, left: Granny and her Auntie Michelle outside of Michelle's trailer home after Granny moved in with Michelle and out of the Delta.

351, right: Grandson Main listening as Lalee describes his constantly changing living situation and the lack of a father who will claim responsibility for him.

352, left: Two of Granny's school mates celebrate Granny's 12th birthday.

352, right: Lalee after hearing that her son, Eddie Reed, has been sent to the penitentiary, without bail.

353, Main after bringing home a failing report card.

354 - 357, From *The Beales of Grey Gardens*, 2006, a compilation of newly edited material from the outtakes of the film *Grey Gardens*. Here Little Edie leaves her reclusive abode to get some sun and take a swim at an East Hampton beach, a short walk from Grey Gardens. Cinematography by Albert Maysles.

358 - 361, *Sleep*, a series of photographs by Albert Maysles, circa 1983 - 1987. Albert's children, Rebekah, Philip and Sara.

filmography

1955
Psychiatry in Russia
Producer: NBC-TV
Director: Albert Maysles
Cinematography:
Albert Maysles
16mm, 1.33:1, black and white
12 minutes

1956
Russian Close-Up
Producer: Albert Maysles
Director: Albert Maysles
Cinematography: Albert Maysles
Sound: Albert Maysles
Editing: Albert Maysles
16mm, 1.33:1, black and white
33 minutes

1958
Youth In Poland (unfinished)
Producer: Albert Maysles,
David Maysles
Director: Albert Maysles,
David Maysles
Cinematography:
Albert Maysles
Sound: David Maysles
16mm, 1.33:1, black and white

1960
Safari Ya Gari
Producer: Albert Maysles
Director: Albert Maysles
Cinematography:
Albert Maysles
Sound: Jerry Feil
Editing: Nell Cox
16mm, 1.33:1, black and white
8 minutes

1963
Showman
Producer: Albert Maysles,
David Maysles
Director: Albert Maysles,
David Maysles
Cinematography:
Albert Maysles
Sound: David Maysles
Editing: Danny Williams,
Tom Bywaters, Betsy Powell
16mm, 1.33:1, black and white
53 minutes

Curtis Jones: An American in Paris (unfinished)
Producer: Albert Maysles,
David Maysles
Director: Albert Maysles,
David Maysles
Cinematography:
Albert Maysles
Sound: David Maysles
16mm, 1.33:1, black and white

1964
*What's Happening!
The Beatles in the U.S.A*
Producer: Granada TV (UK)
Director: Albert Maysles,
David Maysles
Cinematography:
Albert Maysles
Sound: David Maysles
Editing: Danny Williams
16mm, 1.33:1,
black and white
74 minutes

1965
Meet Marlon Brando
Producer: Albert Maysles,
David Maysles
Director: Albert Maysles,
David Maysles
Cinematography:
Albert Maysles
Sound: David Maysles
Editing: Charlotte Zwerin
16mm, 1.33:1, black and white
29 minutes

1966
With Love From Truman
AKA *A Visit With
Truman Capote*
Producer: WNET-TV, David
Maysles, Albert Maysles,
Charlotte Zwerin
Director: David Maysles,
Albert Maysles
Cinematography:
Albert Maysles
Sound: David Maysles
Editing: Charlotte Zwerin
16mm, 1.33:1, black and white
29 minutes

Orson Welles in Spain
(unfinished)
Producer: Albert Maysles,
David Maysles
Director: Albert Maysles,
David Maysles
Cinematography:
Albert Maysles
Sound: David Maysles
Editing: Charlotte Zwerin
16mm, 1.33:1, color
9 minutes (rough assembly)

1968
Salesman
Producer: David Maysles,
Albert Maysles
Director: David Maysles,
Albert Maysles,
Charlotte Zwerin
Cinematography:
Albert Maysles
Sound: David Maysles
Editing: Charlotte Zwerin
16mm, 1.33:1, black and white
91 minutes

Mother (unfinished)
Producer: Albert Maysles,
David Maysles
Director: Albert Maysles,
David Maysles
Cinematography:
Albert Maysles
Sound: David Maysles
16mm, 1.33:1, black and white

1970
Gimme Shelter
Producer: David Maysles,
Albert Maysles
Director: David Maysles,
Albert Maysles,
Charlotte Zwerin
Cinematography:
Albert Maysles, Peter Adair,
Baird Bryant, Joan Churchill,
Ron Dorfman, Robert Elfstrom,
Elliot Erwitt, Bob Fiori,
Adam Giffard, William Kaplan,
Kevin Keating,
Stephen Lighthill,
George Lucas, Jim Moody,
Jack Newman, Pekke Niemela,
Robert Primes, Eric Saarinen,

Peter Smokler, Paul Ryan,
Coulter Watt, Gary Weiss,
Bill Yarhaus, Ed Lachman
Sound: David Maysles,
Michael Becker,
John Brumbaugh,
Howard Chesley,
Pepper Crawford,
Stanley Cronquist,
Paul Deason, Tom Goodwin,
Peter Pilafin, Orly Lindgren,
Walter Murch, Art Rochester,
Nelson Stoll, David Thompson,
Alvin Tokunow, Stanley
Goldstein, Francis Daniel
Editing: Charlotte Zwerin,
Ellen Giffard, Robert Farren,
Joanne Burke, Kent McKinney
16mm, 1.33:1, color
91 mins

1973
Christo's Valley Curtain
Producer: Albert Maysles,
David Maysles
Director: Albert Maysles,
David Maysles, Ellen Giffard
Cinematography:
Albert Maysles
Sound: David Maysles,
Charles Groesbeek
Editing: Ellen Giffard,
Susan Froemke
16mm, 1.33:1, color
28 minutes

1974
The Burks of Georgia
AKA *The Burk Family
of Georgia*
Producer: PBS-TV (for the *Six
American Families* series)
Director: David Maysles,
Albert Maysles, Ellen Hovde,
Muffie Meyer
Cinematography:
Albert Maysles
Sound: David Maysles
Editing: Ellen Hovde,
Muffie Meyer
16mm, 1.33:1, color
53 minutes

1975

Grey Gardens
Producer: Albert Maysles,
David Maysles
Director: David Maysles,
Albert Maysles, Ellen Hovde,
Muffie Meyer, Susan Froemke
Cinematography:
Albert Maysles
Sound: David Maysles
Editing: Ellen Hovde,
Muffie Meyer, Susan Froemke
16mm, 1.33:1, color
94 minutes

1978

Running Fence
Producer: Albert Maysles,
David Maysles
Director: David Maysles,
Charlotte Zwerin,
Albert Maysles
Cinematography:
Albert Maysles
Sound: David Maysles
Editing: Charlotte Zwerin
16mm, 1.33:1, color
58 minutes

1980

Muhammad and Larry
Producer: Marvin Towns,
Clifford Towns, Keith R. Vyse
Director: Albert Maysles,
David Maysles
Cinematography:
Albert Maysles
Sound: David Maysles
Editing: Kate Hirson,
Janet Swanson
16mm, 1.33:1, color
26 minutes

1985

Ozawa
Producer: CBS/Sony Classical,
Peter Gelb, Susan Froemke
Director: David Maysles,
Albert Maysles,
Susan Froemke,
Deborah Dickson
Cinematography:
Albert Maysles,
Robert Leacock, Bob Richman
Sound: David Maysles

Editing: Deborah Dickson
16mm, 1.33:1, color
57 minutes

Vladimir Horowitz:
The Last Romantic
Producer: CBS/Sony,
Peter Gelb, Susan Froemke
Director: David Maysles,
Albert Maysles, Susan
Froemke, Deborah Dickson,
Pat Jaffe
Cinematography:
Albert Maysles , Don Lenzer
Sound: David Maysles,
Michael Shoskes
Editing: Deborah Dickson,
Pat Jaffe
16mm, 1.33:1, color
88 minutes

1986

Islands
Producer: Susan Froemke,
Joel Hinman
Director: Albert Maysles,
Charlotte Zwerin,
David Maysles
Cinematography:
Albert Maysles, Bob Richman,
Erich Roland, Jeff Simon,
Jeff Peterson
Sound: David Maysles
Editing: Kate Hirson
16mm, 1.33:1, color
57 minutes

1987

Horowitz Plays Mozart
Producer: CBS/Sony Classical,
Susan Froemke, Peter Gelb
Director: Albert Maysles,
Susan Froemke,
Charlotte Zwerin
Cinematography:
Albert Maysles, Vic Losick,
Don Lenzer, George Bottos
Sound: Peter Miller,
Gianfranco Cabiddo,
Judy Benjamin
Editing: Pam Wise
16mm, 1.33:1, color
50 minutes

1989

Jessye Norman Sings Carmen
Producer: CBS/Sony,
Peter Gelb, Susan Froemke
Director: Susan Froemke,
Peter Gelb, Albert Maysles,
Charlotte Zwerin
Cinematography:
Albert Maysles, Martin Schaer
Sound: Martin Müller
Editing: Charlotte Zwerin,
Bernadine Colish
16mm, 1.33:1, color
57 minutes

1990

Christo in Paris
Producer: Albert Maysles,
David Maysles, Susan Froemke
Director: David Maysles,
Albert Maysles, Deborah
Dickson, Susan Froemke
Cinematography:
Albert Maysles, Don Lenzer,
Bruce Perlman
Sound: David Maysles
Editing: Deborah Dickson
16mm, 1.33:1, color
58 minutes

1991

Soldiers of Music:
Rostropovitch Returns
to Russia
Producer: CBS/Sony Classical,
Susan Froemke, Peter Gelb
Director: Susan Froemke,
Peter Gelb, Albert Maysles,
Bob Eisenhardt
Cinematography:
Albert Maysles, Ed Lachman,
Wolfgang Becker,
Martin Schaer
Sound: Martin Mueller
Editing: Bob Eisenhardt
16mm, 1.33:1, color
88 minutes

1992

Abortion: Desperate Choices
Producer: HBO Films,
Susan Froemke, Nell Archer
Director: Susan Froemke,
Deborah Dickson,
Albert Maysles

Filming Team: Albert Maysles,
Susan Froemke
Sound Editor: Janet Swanson
Editing: Deborah Dickson
16mm, 1.33:1, color
67 minutes

Baroque Duet
Producer: CBS/Sony Classical,
Maysles Films-Froemke,
Peter Gelb
Director: Susan Froemke,
Peter Gelb, Albert Maysles,
Pat Jaffe
Cinematography: Albert
Maysles, Don Lenzer, Bob
Richman, Greg Andracke,
Jean de Segonzac
Sound: Roger Phenix, Larry
Loewinger, Kenneth Love
Editing: Pat Jaffe
16mm, 1.33:1, color
78 minutes

1994

Accent on the Offbeat
Producer: CBS/Sony Classical,
Susan Froemke, Peter Gelb
Director: Deborah Dickson,
Susan Froemke, Peter Gelb,
Albert Maysles
Cinematography:
Albert Maysles
Editing: Deborah Dickson
16mm, 1.33:1, color
56 minutes

Umbrellas
Producer: Henry Corra
Director: Henry Corra,
Grahame Weinbren,
Albert Maysles
Cinematography:
Albert Maysles,
Robert Richman, Gary Steele,
Robert Leacock,
Don Lenzer, Richard Pearce,
Martin Schaer
Sound: Merce Williams,
Ronald Yoshida, Peter Miller,
Bruce Perlman, Roger Phenix
Editing: Grahame Weinbren,
Sakae Ishikawa
16mm, 1.33:1, color
81 minutes

filmography

1996
Letting Go: A Hospice Journey
Producer: HBO Films,
Susan Froemke
Director: Susan Froemke,
Deborah Dickson,
Albert Maysles
Cinematography:
Albert Maysles
Sound: L. Mark Sorre
Editing: Deborah Dickson
16mm, 1.33:1, color
90 minutes

1997
Concert of Wills:
Making of the Getty Center
Producer: Susan Froemke
Director: Susan Froemke, Bob
Eisenhardt, Albert Maysles
Cinematography:
Albert Maysles,
Christophe Lanzenberg,
Christian Blackwood,
Robert Richman,
Giorgio Urbinelli
Sound: Bruce Perlman,
Michael Reily
Editing: Bob Eisenhardt
16mm, 1.33:1, color
100 minutes

2001
Lalee's Kin:
The Legacy of Cotton
Producer: HBO Films,
Susan Froemke
Director: Susan Froemke,
Deborah Dickson,
Albert Maysles
Cinematography:
Albert Maysles, Jim Dollarhide
Sound: Peter Miller, Donald
Thomas, Margaret Crimmins,
Greg Smith
Editing: Deborah Dickson
16mm, 1.33:1, color
88 minutes

With The Filmmaker:
Portraits by Albert Maysles
(Four episodes: Wes Anderson,
Robert Duvall, Jane Campion,
Martin Scorsese)
Producer: IFC Channel,

Antonio Ferrera,
Larry Kamerman,
Rebecca Losick
Director: Albert Maysles,
Antonio Ferrera,
Larry Kamerman
Cinematography:
Albert Maysles
Sound: Antonio Ferrera
Editing: Matt Prinzing
Digital video, 1.33:1, color
30 mins (each episode)

2005
Sean O'Casey: Under a
Coloured Cap
Producer: Mary Beth Yarrow
Director: Shivaun O' Casey
Writers: Shivaun O' Casey,
Mary Beth Yarrow
Cinematography: Albert
Maysles
Editing: Guy Crossman
Sound: Antonio Ferrera
Digital Video, 1.33:1, color
60 Minutes

2006
In Good Conscience
Producer: Barbara Rick
Director: Barbara Rick
Cinematography:
Albert Maysles
Editing: Spiro C. Lampros
Sound: Jim Anderson
Digital Video, 1.33:1, color
82 minutes

2006
Ida, Ella & Willa
(from the omnibus film
Time Piece)
Producer: Neda Armian,
Margaret Bodde, Sadie Tillery
Director: Albert Maysles
Cinematography:
Albert Maysles
Digital video, 1.33:1, color
10 minutes

The Beales of Grey Gardens
Producer: Tanja Meding
Director: Albert Maysles,
David Maysles,
Ian Markiewicz

Cinematography:
Albert Maysles
Sound: David Maysles
Editing: Michael Hession
16mm, 1.33:1, color
90 minutes

2007
The Gates
Producer: Maureen Ryan,
Antonio Ferrera,
Vladimir Yavachev
Director: Antonio Ferrera,
Albert Maysles,
David Maysles, Matt Prinzing
Cinematography:
Albert Maysles,
Antonio Ferrera, Peter Hutton
Sound: David Maysles,
Antonio Ferrera
Editing: Antonio Ferrera,
Matt Prinzing
16mm/DV/HD, 1.85:1, color
90 minutes

Sally Gross:
The Pleasure of Stillness
Producer: Tanja Meding
Director: Albert Maysles,
Kristen Nutile
Cinematography:
Albert Maysles, Kristen Nutile,
Sean Williams,
Greg Vanderveer,
Peter Goodman,
Michael Hosenfeld,
Anne Alvergue
Sound: Andres Arredondo
Editing: Kristen Nutile
Digital video, 1.33:1, color
56 minutes

1957
Poland 'Outlook'
Producer:
NBC-TV, Frank Reuven
Director:
Frank Reuven, Chet Huntley
Cinematography:
Albert Maysles

16mm, 1.33:1, black and white
30 minutes

1960
Primary
Producer: Robert Drew,
Time-Life, Inc.
Executive Producer:
Robert Drew
Cinematography:
Richard Leacock,
Albert Maysles,
Terrence McCartney-Filgate,
D.A. Pennebaker
Sound: Robert Drew
Editing: Robert Drew,
Richard Leacock,
D.A. Pennebaker,
Terrence McCartney-Filgate,
Robert Farren
16mm, 1.33:1, black and white
53 minutes

On the Pole
Producer: Robert Drew,
Time-Life, Inc.
Executive Producer:
Robert Drew
Cinematography:
D.A. Pennebaker, William Ray,
Abbott Mills, Albert Maysles
Sound: Robert Drew
Editing: Robert Drew
16mm, 1.33:1, black and white
52 mins.

1961
Yanki, No!
Producer: Drew Associates,
ABC-TV
Executive Producer:
Robert Drew
Cinematography:
Richard Leacock,
D.A. Pennebaker,
Albert Maysles
Sound: Robert Drew
Editing: Robert Drew
16mm, 1.33:1, black and white
60 minutes

Kenya
Part I:
Land of the White Ghost
Part II:

Land of the Black Ghost
Producer: Robert Drew,
ABC-TV, Time-Life, Inc.
Executive Producer:
Richard Leacock
Cinematography:
Richard Leacock,
Albert Maysles
Sound: Gregory Shuker
Editing: Robert Drew
16mm, 1.33:1, black and white
60 minutes

X-Pilot
Producer: Drew Associates,
Time-Life, Inc., ABC-TV
Executive Producer:
Robert Drew
Cinematography:
Albert Maysles,
Terence McCartney-Filgate
Sound: Howard Sochurek,
Gregory Shuker
Editing: Robert Drew
16mm, 1:33:1, black and white
25 minutes

*Adventures on the
New Frontier*
Producer: Drew Associates,
Time-Life, Inc.
Executive Producer:
Robert Drew
Cinematography:
Richard Leacock,
D.A. Pennebaker, Albert
Maysles, Kenneth Snelson
Sound: Robert Drew, Lee Hall,
Gregory Shuker,
David Maysles
Editing: Robert Drew
16mm, 1.33:1, black and white
52 minutes

1962
Anastasia
Producer:
NBC-TV, Bo Goldman
Director: Albert Maysles,
David Maysles
Cinematography:
Albert Maysles
Sound: David Maysles
16mm, 1.33:1, black and white
12 minutes

1963
*Carl Sandburg Reads from
"Honey & Salt"*
Director: Albert Maysles,
David Maysles
Cinematography:
Albert Maysles
Sound: David Maysles
16mm, 1.33:1, black and white
3 minutes

At Home with Life
Producer: Life Magazine
Director: Albert Maysles,
David Maysles
Cinematography:
Albert Maysles
Sound: David Maysles
16mm, 1.33:1, color
14 minutes

The Theater of Tomorrow
Producer: ABC-TV, Robert
Saudek, Mary Ahern
Director: Michael Ritchie
Cinematography: Albert
Maysles
16mm, 1.33:1, black and white
60 minutes

1964
IBM: A Self Portrait
Producer: Irving Gitlin
Director: Albert Maysles,
David Maysles
Cinematography:
Albert Maysles
Sound: David Maysles
Editing: Danny Williams,
Kate Glidden
16mm, 1.33:1, black and white
30 minutes

*Employee Barriers to
Good Service*
Producer: Bell Telephone,
Stanley Hirson
Director: Albert Maysles,
David Maysles
Cinematography:
Albert Maysles
Sound: David Maysles
Editing: Kate Glidden
16mm, 1.33:1, black and white,
12 minutes

1965
Montparnesse-Levallois
(From the omnibus film
Paris vu par. . .)
Producer: Barbet Schroeder,
Films du Losange
Director: Jean-Luc Godard
Cinematography: Albert
Maysles, Néstor Almendros
Sound: René Levert
Editing: Jacqueline Raynal
16mm, 1.33:1, color
12 minutes

*Sean O'Casey:
The Spirit of Ireland*
Producer: 20th Century Fox
Director: Albert Maysles,
David Maysles
Cinematography:
Albert Maysles
Sound: David Maysles
Editing: Elliot P. Geisinger
16mm, 1.33:1, black and white
8 minutes

20th Century Fox Press Junket
Producer: 20th Century Fox
Director: Albert Maysles,
David Maysles
Cinematography:
Albert Maysles
Sound: David Maysles
16mm, 1.33:1, black and white
20 minutes

Bill Blass
Producer: Benton & Bowles
Director: Albert Maysles,
David Maysles
Cinematography:
Albert Maysles
Sound: David Maysles
16mm, 1.33:1, black and white
8 minutes

Cut Piece
Producer: Yoko Ono
Director: Albert Maysles,
David Maysles
Cinematography:
Albert Maysles
Sound: David Maysles
16mm, 1.33:1, black and white
9 minutes

1966
Dali's Fantastic Dream
Producer: 20th Century Fox
Director: Albert Maysles,
David Maysles
Cinematography:
Albert Maysles
Sound: David Maysles
16mm, 1.33:1, black and white
8 minutes

Who is Jean Shrimpton?
Producer: Granada TV
Director: Dick Fontaine
Cinematography:
Albert Maysles,
David Samuelson
Sound: David Maysles
16mm, 1.33:1, black and white
30 minutes

MGM Press Junket
Producer: Metro,
Goldwyn & Mayer
Director: Albert Maysles,
David Maysles
Cinematography:
Albert Maysles
Sound: David Maysles
16mm, 1.33:1, black and white
20 minutes

1967
'Tony Rome' Featurette
Producer: 20th Century Fox
Director: Albert Maysles,
David Maysles
Cinematography:
Albert Maysles
Sound: David Maysles
16mm, 1.33:1, color
8 minutes

Problem On Our Hands
Producer: Johnson & Johnson,
Stanley Hirson
Director: Albert Maysles,
David Maysles
Cinematography:
Albert Maysles
Sound: David Maysles
Editing: Edward Packer
16mm, 1.33:1,
color/black and white
20 minutes

1968

Monterey Pop
Producer:
Leacock-Pennebaker Films
Director: D.A. Pennebaker
Cinematography:
D.A. Pennebaker, Nick Doob,
Barry Feinstein, Albert Maysles,
Richard Leacock, Roger Murphy,
Nick Proferes, James Desmond
Sound: Wally Heider,
Robert Van Dyke, John Cooke
Editing: Nina Schulman,
Mary Lampson
16mm, 1.33:1, color
78 minutes

A Journey To Jerusalem
Producer: Michael Mindlin, Jr.
Director: Michael Mindlin, Jr.
Cinematography:
Albert Maysles, Richard
Leacock, Stan Hirson,
Bruce Martin, Sid Reichman,
Joe Ryan
Sound: David Maysles
Editing: Robert Farren,
Dorothy Tod, Isaac Cohen
16mm, 1.33:1, color
86 minutes

Emergency: The Living Theatre
Producer: Gwen Brown,
Julian Beck, Judith Malina
Director: Gwen Brown
Cinematography:
Albert Maysles,
Alan Raymond, Frank Simon
Editing: Dan Halas
16mm, 1.33:1, black and white
29 minutes

1970

Reflections
Producer: Japan Airlines
Director: Nell Cox
Cinematography:
Albert Maysles
Sound: Vic Losick
Editing: Nell Cox
16mm, 1.33:1, color
26 minutes

1971

Grand Funk Railroad:
Live at Shea Stadium
Producer: Terry Knight
Director: Albert Maysles,
David Maysles
Cinematography:
Albert Maysles,
Richard Leacock,
Robert Van Dyke
Sound: David Maysles,
Robert Van Dyke
Editing: Muffie Meyer
16mm, 1.33:1, color
50 minutes

1973

Sisters (unfinished)
Producer: Peter Beard,
Lee Radziwill
Director: David Maysles,
Albert Maysles
Cinematography:
Albert Maysles
Sound: David Maysles
16mm, 1.33:1, color

1974

'Conrack' Featurette
Producer: 20th Century Fox
Director: Albert Maysles,
David Maysles
Cinematography:
Albert Maysles
Sound: David Maysles
16mm, 1.33:1, color
9 minutes

1977

The Grateful Dead Movie
Producer: Ron Rakow,
Eddie Washington
Director: Jerry Garcia,
Leon Gast
Cinematography:
Stephen Lighthill,
David Myers, Albert Maysles,
Robert Primes
Sound: Pat Jackson
Editing: Susan Crutcher,
John Nutt, Jerry Garcia,
Lisa Fruchtman
16mm, 1.33:1, color
131 minutes

1978

Diane Von Furstenberg:
A Designer's Touch
Producer: Sears & Roebuck
Director: David Maysles,
Albert Maysles
Cinematography:
Albert Maysles
Sound: David Maysles
16mm, 1.33:1, color
12 minutes

1979

Smirnoff Style
Producer: Smirnoff
Director: Albert Maysles,
David Maysles
Cinematography:
Albert Maysles
Sound: David Maysles
16mm, 1.33:1, color
22 minutes

1981

Good Living with
Martha Stewart
Producer: Dan Cooper
Director: David Maysles,
Albert Maysles
Cinematography:
Albert Maysles
Sound: David Maysles
16mm, 1.33:1, color
25 minutes

1983

Bob Dylan: "Don't Fall
Apart on Me Tonight" &
"License to Kill"
(unfinished music shorts)
Producer: Sony Music
Cinematography:
Albert Maysles
16mm, 1.33:1, color
10 minutes (total)

1985

Chase Manhattan Bank:
The Beginning
Producer:
Chase Manhattan Bank
Director: David Maysles,
Albert Maysles
Cinematography:
Albert Maysles

Sound: David Maysles
16mm, 1.33:1, color
11 minutes

1989

The Met in Japan
Producer: CBS/Sony Classical,
Peter Gelb, Susan Froemke
Director: Susan Froemke,
Albert Maysles
Cinematography:
Albert Maysles
Editing: Deborah Dickson
16mm, 1.33:1, color
21 minutes

Sports Illustrated Swimsuit '89
Producer: Susan Froemke
Director: Susan Froemke,
Albert Maysles
Cinematography:
Albert Maysles,
Dyanna Taylor,
Alexander Gruszynski
Editing: Geof Bartz,
Bob Eisenhardt, Pam Wise
16mm, 1.33:1, color
55 minutes

1991

Down to Earth:
Farmers on Farming
Producer: DuPont Classic
Director: Henry Corra,
Albert Maysles
Cinematography:
Albert Maysles
16mm, 1.33:1, color
10 minutes

1992

Sports Illustrated Swimsuit '92
Producer: Susan Froemke
Director: Susan Froemke,
Albert Maysles
Cinematography:
Albert Maysles,
Dyanna Taylor, Christian
Blackwood,
Christophe Lanzenberg
Editing: Jay Freund,
Kathy Dougherty, Juliet Weber
16mm, 1.33:1, color
57 minutes

1993
Sports Illustrated Swimsuit '93
Producer: Susan Froemke
Director: Susan Froemke,
Kathy Dougherty,
Albert Maysles
Cinematography:
Albert Maysles,
Dyanna Taylor,
Douglas Cooper,
Christophe Lanzenberg,
Gary Steele
Editing: Kathy Dougherty,
Bob Eisenhardt
16mm, 1.33:1, color
43 minutes

1994
Conversations With The Rolling Stones
Producer: Susan Froemke
Director: Susan Froemke,
Kathy Dougherty,
Albert Maysles
Cinematography:
Adam Kimmel, Albert Maysles
Editing: Kathy Dougherty
Sound: Ross Redfern
16mm, 1.33:1,
black and white, color
23 mins

1996
When We Were Kings
Producer: Leon Gast,
David Sonenberg
Director: Leon Gast
Cinematography:
Albert Maysles,
Maryse Alberti,
Paul Goldsmith,
Kevin Keating, Roderick Young
Sound: Gary Kelgern,
Robert Cardelli, Chris Stone
Editing: Leon Gast,
Taylor Hackford, Jeffrey Levy-Hinte, Keith Robinson
35mm, 1.85:1, color
89 minutes

Christo & Jeanne-Claude Wrapped Reichstag, Berlin 1971- 95
Producer: Arte, ZDF, Ex-Nihilo
Director: Jörg-Daniel Hissen,

Wolfram Hissen
Cinematography:
Michael Hammon,
Albert Maysles, Eric Turpin,
Jörg Widmer
Editing: Dirk Grau,
Götz Filenius
35mm, 1.85:1, color
98 minutes

2002
Stages: Britney Spears
Producer: Jim Forni
Director: Judy Hoffman
Cinematography:
Albert Maysles, Antonio
Ferrera, Judy Hoffman,
Jim Morrissette
Digital video, 1.33:1, color
60 minutes

2005
Stolen
Producer: Jen Kaczor,
Sally Jo Fifer
Director: Rebecca Dreyfus
Cinematography:
Albert Maysles,
Rebecca Dreyfus
Editor: Liz Ludden,
Markus A. Peters,
Kate Taverna
Digital video, 1.33:1, color
90 minutes

2006
Not A Photograph: The Mission of Burma Story
Producer: Eran Lobel
Director: Jeffrey Iwanicki,
David A. Kleiler, Jr.
Cinematography:
Albert Maysles,
W. Mott Hupfel III,
Leif Husted-Jensen
Editor: Tyler Hubby,
Jeffrey Iwanicki,
Anne Renehan,
Christopher Santo,
John Suvannavejh
Digital video, 1.33:1, color

When the Road Bends: Tales of a Gypsy Caravan
Producer: Jasmine Dellal,
Wouter Barendrecht
Director: Jasmine Dellal
Cinematography:
Albert Maysles,
Alain de Halleux
Sound: Mariusz Glabinski
Editor: Margarita Jimeno,
Paulo Padilha
Digital video, 1.33:1, color
110 minutes

2007
Addiction
(segment, *A Mother's Desperation*)
Producer: HBO,
Susan Froemke
Director: Susan Froemke,
Albert Maysles
Cinematography:
Albert Maysles
Editing: Paula Heredia
Digital video, 1.33:1, color
86 minutes
(total running time)

acknowledgements

The author and editors wish to gratefully acknowledge the following individuals, without whose talents, efforts, and support this book would have been impossible.

Firstly, we give very special thanks to our assistant editors Sean Williams, Molly Fair, and Ian Markiewicz. Their prodigious efforts to catalog and preserve the contents of the Maysles Films archive and their astute selections have greatly benefited the range and quality of this book.

This book is marked by the influence of a great many people who helped in guiding its conception. For lending their intelligence and indefatigable support: Bill Brand, Gillian Walker, Gerald O'Grady, Mark McElhatten, Aaron Bremmer, Jonas Herbsman, Kent Jones, Sherry Daly, Pat Jones, Bruce Davidson, John Hoffman, Martin Scorsese, Kevin Hooper, Anne and Robert Drew, Richard Leher, Laura Coxson, and the entire staff of Maysles Films, Inc.

Steve would like to thank Timothy Greenfield-Sanders and Liliana Greenfield-Sanders for introducing him to Al Maysles and deepening his understanding of Al's work. And thanks to Maria Stenina and Ann Prentnieks for technical assistance.

At Steidl, we would like to thank especially Jonas Wettre, Julia Braun, Michael Mack and Gerhard. Mark Michaelson's skill and brilliance in design has made this book a thing of beauty. We are indebted to him.

This book stands as a tribute to the many talented cinematographers, photographers and editors who have played an indispensable part in the history of Maysles Films. The captions and filmography that conclude this volume are an attempt to record as accurately as possible the individuals who, under the aegis of Maysles Films, worked with Al in the creation of many of the company's most important works. We salute them for their creative energies in bringing the films into existence. Any errors or omissions are solely our own, for which we ask forgiveness.

colophon

Copublished by Steven Kasher Gallery, New York
and Steidl Publishers, Göttingen, Germany

First edition 2007

© 2007 for the text by the authors
© 2007 Maysles Films Inc. and the credited photographers for the images
© for this edition: Steidl Publishers, Göttingen and
   Steven Kasher Gallery, New York

Book design by Steven Kasher and Mark Michaelson

Scans done by Maysles Films Inc.
Production and printing by Steidl, Göttingen

Steven Kasher Gallery
521 West 23rd Street
New York, NY 10011
www.stevenkasher.com
Phone +212-966 3978

Steidl
Düstere Str. 4/ D-37073 Göttingen
Phone +49 551-49 60 60/ Fax +49 551-49 60 649
E-mail: mail@steidl.de
www.steidlville.com/www.steidl.de

ISBN 978-3-86521-496-6

Printed in Germany